The V-ZUG Adora SLQ

V-ZUG Ltd. Switzerland has once again proven its superiority in its work with water and ensures a quantum leap in the act of doing laundry with its groundbreaking innovations.

V-ZUG's WetClean setting rings in a new era of doing laundry and ensures the ultimate care for the favorite clothes in your closet. Its completely new technology with a separate, internal circulation circuit and sophisticated dispersion nozzles ensures the unequalled delicate and gentle cleaning of your clothes, which are gently moved back and forth. The V-ZUG WetClean setting is an extremely gentle, professional cleaning process, almost like a wellness program for sensitive textiles.

Steam anti-crease is another step towards a new, more convenient era of doing laundry. The Adora SLQ is the first washing machine to uncrease laundry using steam – so thoroughly that it usually makes ironing unnecessary.

The new Adora SLQ isn't just a huge help, it also doesn't make any noise. Because, thanks to the world-exclusive **Vibration Absorbing System (VAS)**, the machine runs completely concentrically and vibration-free!

The Swiss Leader

www.vzug.com.au

ABC

delicious.
comfort

SOUPS • PIES • ROASTS • PASTA • PUDDINGS

contents.

SOUPS	8
STARTERS	20
PIES	28
BRAISES	40
WEEKNIGHTS	56
ROASTS	66
PASTA	74
SPICE	86
BAKES	98
SIDES	106
SWEET PIES & TARTS	116
PUDDINGS	126
BASICS	136
RECIPE INDEX	137

welcome.

Growing up in England, I have a special connection with the cooler months of the year and the comfort food that goes with them. Surely there's nothing better than coming in from the cold to the glorious aroma of food gently simmering on the stovetop, or a fragrant pudding baking in the oven.

delicious. Comfort is a celebration of some of our favourite recipes, and plenty of new ones, that are guaranteed to beat the chill. Inside you'll find everything from steaming bowls of soup to warming casseroles, hearty pastas and bakes, quick midweek meals and sweet pies and tarts.

Whether you're gathered around the table with family and friends, or snuggled in front of the fire with dinner on your lap, you're guaranteed to find something in *delicious. Comfort* that you'll enjoy making – and eating every last morsel!

Happy cooking,

Valli

Valli Little, Food Director

Roast capsicum & tomato soup

soups

11 homestyle minestrone
11 roast capsicum & tomato soup
11 thai-style butternut pumpkin soup with prawns
12 chicken, barley & vegetable soup
12 ploughman's soup
15 fennel soup with winter greens and bacon
15 mexican chilli con carne soup
16 pea, ham & sausage soup
16 cauliflower cheese soup
19 moroccan spiced soup with jewelled couscous
19 hot and sour prawn soup

Thai-style butternut pumpkin soup with prawns

Roast capsicum & tomato soup

soups.

homestyle minestrone
Serves 6
Soak the soup beans a day ahead.

250g dried Italian soup bean mix*, soaked overnight in cold water
¼ cup (60ml) extra virgin olive oil
1 large onion, finely chopped
1 garlic clove, finely chopped
2 celery stalks, finely chopped
2 carrots, finely chopped
100g sliced pancetta, chopped
2 tbs tomato paste
400g can chopped tomatoes
3L chicken (see Basics, p 136) or vegetable stock
2 bay leaves
1⅔ cups (200g) frozen peas
¼ savoy cabbage, core removed, thinly sliced (to give 1½ cups)
150g ditalini, small macaroni or other short tube pasta
½ cup good-quality basil pesto
Freshly grated parmesan, to serve

Drain soaked beans. Rinse and drain again. Heat the oil in a large, heavy-based saucepan over medium-low heat. Add the onion, garlic, celery, carrot and pancetta and cook, stirring, for 10 minutes or until the vegetables have softened. Add tomato paste and stir for a further minute. Add beans, tomatoes, stock and bay leaves. Increase heat to high and bring to the boil, then partially cover, reduce heat to low and simmer, stirring occasionally to prevent catching, for 2 hours or until the beans are tender.

Add the peas, cabbage and pasta, and cook, uncovered, for a further 10 minutes or until the pasta is al dente and the peas and cabbage are tender. Season to taste with salt and pepper (adding salt earlier can make the beans tough). Ladle the minestrone into bowls, then swirl through some pesto and serve topped with parmesan.

* Italian soup beans are available from supermarkets and greengrocers.

roast capsicum & tomato soup
Serves 4

2 red capsicums (about 400g total)
1 tbs olive oil, plus extra to drizzle
1 small onion, chopped
2 garlic cloves, chopped
2 x 400g cans chopped tomatoes
300ml vegetable stock
80g soft goat's cheese
Bread or savoury muffins, to serve

Place the capsicums on a baking sheet under a hot grill and cook until the skin is charred and black. Transfer to a plastic bag, seal and set aside for 10 minutes. Peel off skin, remove and discard the membrane and seeds. Chop and set aside.

Heat the oil in a large saucepan over medium heat. Add onion and cook, stirring, for 1-2 minutes or until softened. Add garlic, tomato, capsicum and stock. Season, bring to the boil, then reduce heat to medium-low and simmer for 5 minutes.

Cool slightly then blend, in batches, in a food processor or using a stick blender until smooth. Return the soup to the pan and reheat over medium-low heat. Season. Ladle the soup into bowls, sprinkle with soft goat's cheese and drizzle with the extra olive oil. Serve with bread or savoury muffins.

thai-style butternut pumpkin soup with prawns
Serves 6

¼ cup (60ml) olive oil
1 onion, finely chopped
1 tsp finely grated ginger
1 tbs finely chopped lemongrass
1 tbs Thai red curry paste
1L (4 cups) chicken stock (see Basics, p 136), heated
1kg butternut pumpkin, peeled, cut into 2cm pieces (750g peeled weight)
2 kaffir lime leaves*
1 cup (250ml) coconut milk
Zest of ½ lime, plus 2 tbs lime juice
12 green king prawns, peeled
1 small red chilli, seeds removed, finely chopped

Heat 1 tbs of oil in a large saucepan over medium heat. Add the onion, ginger and lemongrass and cook for 3-4 minutes until very soft. Add the red curry paste and cook for a further minute until fragrant and the oil separates.

Add the stock, pumpkin and lime leaves and simmer over medium heat for 15-20 minutes until the pumpkin is very tender. Remove from the heat and discard the lime leaves. Stir in the coconut milk. Blend soup, in batches, until smooth. Return to pan and add lime juice. Season to taste and keep hot.

Heat the remaining 2 tbs of oil in a large frypan over medium-high heat. Season the prawns and cook for 1-2 minutes each side until just cooked. Divide the soup among serving bowls and add the prawns. Sprinkle with chopped chilli and lime zest.

* Kaffir lime leaves are available from greengrocers and Asian food shops.

soups.

Chicken, barley & vegetable soup

chicken, barley & vegetable soup
Serves 6

2 tbs olive oil
750g chicken pieces (any mix of thighs, wings or drumsticks)
1 leek (white part only), sliced
1 celery stalk, chopped
1 onion, chopped
1 garlic clove, crushed
1 cup (200g) pearl barley
1 fresh bay leaf
2 carrots, peeled, cut into 2cm pieces
1 turnip, peeled, cut into 2cm pieces
1 cup flat-leaf parsley leaves, chopped, plus extra to garnish

Heat the olive oil in a large saucepan over medium heat. Cook the chicken, in batches, for 6-8 minutes, turning, until browned all over. Remove the chicken and season with sea salt and freshly ground black pepper. Set aside until needed.

Add the leek, celery and onion to the saucepan and gently cook, stirring, for 6 minutes until softened. Stir in the garlic. Return the chicken to the saucepan, pour in 2L (8 cups) water, add the pearl barley, bay leaf, carrot, turnip and chopped parsley and bring to the boil. Skim the surface, then reduce the heat to medium-low and simmer, partially covered, for 1 hour or until the chicken and barley are very tender and the broth is slightly thickened (if necessary, uncover and reduce over a higher heat). Season with sea salt and freshly ground black pepper, then ladle into serving bowls and garnish with chopped parsley.

ploughman's soup
Serves 4-6

2 tbs oil
1 onion, chopped
1 celery stalk, chopped, plus extra celery stalks to serve
1 garlic clove, chopped
50g sliced pancetta, roughly chopped
4 green apples (about 750g total), peeled, cored, chopped
3/4 cup (185ml) dry alcoholic cider
2 cups (500ml) chicken stock (see Basics, p 136)
1 thyme sprig
2 cups (240g) grated mature cheddar, plus extra cheddar to serve
Chopped flat-leaf parsley, to garnish
Crusty bread rolls and chutney, to serve

Heat the oil in a large saucepan over medium heat. Add the onion, celery, garlic and pancetta and gently cook, stirring, for 3-4 minutes until softened slightly but not coloured.

Add the apple and stir to combine, then add the cider, stock and thyme. Bring to the boil over medium-high heat, then reduce heat to low and simmer, partially covered, for 25 minutes until the apple is softened. Remove from heat, add the grated cheddar and stand for 10 minutes.

Discard the thyme sprig, then blend the mixture with a stick blender until smooth (or puree in batches in a blender). Season the soup with sea salt and freshly ground black pepper. Garnish with parsley. Serve with bread, chutney and extra cheddar and celery.

Ploughman's soup

Fennel soup with winter greens and bacon

soups.

fennel soup with winter greens and bacon
Serves 4

150g unsalted butter
2 large leeks (white part only), finely sliced
1 tsp fennel seeds
3 fennel bulbs (about 800g total), coarsely chopped
900g sebago potatoes, peeled, cut into 2cm pieces
1.25L (5 cups) chicken stock (see Basics, p 136), heated
150ml pure (thin) cream
200g savoy cabbage
175g pancetta, chopped
Handful roughly chopped thyme leaves

Melt 100g of the butter in a large saucepan over medium-low heat. Add the leek and gently cook, stirring occasionally, for 10 minutes or until very soft. Add fennel seeds and cook for 2-3 minutes. Stir in fennel and potato.

Cover vegetables with a sheet of wet baking paper and place a lid on pan. Cook gently for 10-12 minutes until vegetables are just tender. Remove and discard the paper. Add the stock, bring to the boil, then cover and simmer for 30 minutes until the vegetables are very tender.

Leave to cool slightly, then pour three-quarters of soup into a food processor or blender and pulse until smooth. Return to the pan, stir in the cream and season. Gently reheat the soup but make sure it doesn't boil.

Meanwhile, discard the tough outer leaves from the cabbage. Roughly tear the remaining leaves, discarding any hard stalks, and blanch them in boiling salted water for 2-3 minutes. Refresh under cold running water and drain.

Melt remaining 50g butter in a large frypan over medium heat. Add the pancetta and cook for 3-4 minutes or until golden. Add the cabbage and thyme and cook, stirring, for about 5 minutes or until cabbage is tender. Season well. Ladle soup into bowls and spoon the cabbage and pancetta into each bowl to serve.

Mexican chilli con carne soup

mexican chilli con carne soup
Serves 4

2 tbs olive oil
1 onion, finely chopped
2 garlic cloves, finely chopped
2 carrots, chopped
1 tsp dried chilli flakes
1 tsp sweet paprika
1 tbs ground cumin
1 tbs ground coriander
3 tbs tomato paste
500g beef mince
1L (4 cups) chicken stock (see Basics, p 136), heated
400g can kidney beans, rinsed, drained
2 corn cobs
Avocado, crusty bread and lemon wedges, to serve

Heat the olive oil in a large saucepan over medium heat. Add the chopped onion, garlic and carrot and cook, stirring, for 6-8 minutes until the onion is soft.

Add the chilli flakes, paprika, ground cumin and ground coriander and stir for 1 minute until fragrant. Stir in the tomato paste and cook, stirring, for 2 minutes.

Add the beef and cook, stirring with a wooden spoon to break it up, for 2 minutes or until the meat starts to colour. Add the chicken stock and simmer, uncovered, for 10 minutes.

Meanwhile, use a sharp knife to remove the kernels from the corn cobs.

Stir in the kidney beans and corn and cook for 2 minutes until heated through. Serve the soup with the avocado, crusty bread and lemon wedges.

soups.

Pea, ham & sausage soup

pea, ham & sausage soup
Serves 6
Soak the split peas a day ahead.

2½ cups (500g) dried green split peas, soaked overnight in cold water
1 tbs olive oil
30g unsalted butter
2 onions, finely chopped
1 carrot, finely chopped
2 celery stalks, finely chopped
2 smoked ham hocks*
1 cup (250ml) dry white wine
1 cup (250ml) chicken (see Basics, p 136) or vegetable stock
2 tsp thyme leaves
2 bay leaves
Grated zest of 1 lemon
150g sour cream
¼ cup flat-leaf parsley, plus extra to serve
8 mixed smoked sausages (such as cabanossi, Vienna frankfurts, bratwurst and kransky)*
Rye bread, to serve

Drain soaked peas. Rinse and drain again.
   Heat the oil and butter in a large, heavy-based pan over medium heat. Add onion, carrot and celery. Cook, stirring, for 5 minutes or until softened. Add ham, peas, wine, stock, herbs, zest and 1.5L (6 cups) water. Bring to the boil over medium-high heat, skimming any foam on surface. Reduce heat to low. Simmer, partially covered, for 2 hours until ham and peas are tender, stirring occasionally to prevent catching and topping up with water if it's becoming too thick. Remove ham from soup. Cool, then peel and shred meat, discarding skin and bone.
   Stir sour cream and parsley into soup. If you prefer a smoother soup, cool slightly then puree half in a blender. Return to pan with ham and heat through.
   Meanwhile, cook sausages in boiling water for 2-3 minutes to heat through. Drain and transfer to a plate. Slice some sausages. Serve soup topped with sliced sausages and extra parsley, with whole sausages and rye bread on the side.
* From delis and butchers.

cauliflower cheese soup
Serves 4-6

50g unsalted butter
1 onion, chopped
1 garlic clove, chopped
2 potatoes (about 300g total), peeled, cut into 2cm pieces
1L (4 cups) chicken stock (see Basics, p 136) or vegetable stock, heated
1.5kg cauliflower, broken into florets
½ cup (125ml) pure (thin) cream
100g mature cheddar, grated
125g gruyere cheese, grated
Roughly chopped flat-leaf parsley leaves, to garnish

Melt the butter in a large saucepan over medium heat. Add the onion and garlic and cook, stirring, for 5 minutes or until softened. Add the potato, stock and half the cauliflower. Season. Bring to the boil, then reduce the heat slightly and simmer for 20 minutes until very soft. Cool slightly.
   Meanwhile, blanch the remaining cauliflower in boiling salted water for 6 minutes or until just tender. Drain, refresh under cold water and drain again.
   Blend the soup, in batches, in a food processor or blender until smooth. Return to the clean saucepan. Add the cream and season to taste, then gently reheat until hot but not boiling. Add the blanched cauliflower and heat through.
   Preheat the grill to high. Ladle the soup into 4 shallow heatproof bowls. Mix the cheeses together and scatter over the soup. Stand the bowls on a baking tray and grill for 2-3 minutes until the cheese has melted and is turning golden. (Take care when handling the hot bowls.) Garnish with chopped parsley leaves.

Cauliflower cheese soup

Moroccan spiced soup with jewelled couscous

soups.

moroccan spiced soup with jewelled couscous
Serves 6

2 tbs olive oil
450g rump or sirloin steak, trimmed, cut into 2-3cm pieces
2 small onions, chopped
2 garlic cloves, crushed
1 carrot, finely chopped
2 celery stalks, chopped
1 tbs harissa*, plus extra to serve
2 tsp plain flour
1.25L (5 cups) vegetable or beef stock (see Basics, p 136), heated
400g can chopped tomatoes
75g dried apricots
1 butternut pumpkin, peeled, cut into 2cm pieces

Jewelled couscous
85g couscous
150ml vegetable stock, heated
1 tomato, seeds removed, chopped
2 tbs chopped mint leaves

Heat the oil in a heavy-based pan over medium-high heat. Add beef and cook for 5 minutes or until browned all over. Remove with a slotted spoon. Set aside.

Add the onion and garlic to the pan, reduce the heat slightly and cook for 5 minutes or until softened. Add the carrot and celery, cover and cook for 5 minutes or until the vegetables have softened slightly. Stir in the harissa and flour and cook for 2 minutes. Gradually whisk in the hot stock.

Stir in the tomatoes and apricots, then bring to the boil. Cover and simmer gently for 20 minutes. Season well. Add pumpkin and beef. Cover and cook, stirring occasionally, for 25 minutes or until pumpkin and beef are tender.

Meanwhile, to make jewelled couscous, place couscous in a bowl. Pour over the hot stock, cover and stand for 5 minutes, then fluff up with a fork. Stir in tomatoes and mint. Season. Ladle into bowls, then divide couscous among bowls. Serve with extra harissa on the side.

* A North African chilli paste, from Middle Eastern and gourmet food shops.

Hot and sour prawn soup

hot & sour prawn soup
Serves 4

This fragrant broth is the most famous of Thai soups. Lemongrass and kaffir lime leaves are its main flavours, with a kick of red chilli.

1 tbs tamarind concentrate*
1 tsp sunflower oil
1 tsp grated palm sugar*
2 garlic cloves, finely sliced
1L (4 cups) fish stock*
2 lemongrass stems, outer layer discarded, finely sliced
5cm piece galangal*, peeled, sliced
2 fresh or dried kaffir lime leaves*
1 small red chilli, sliced
250g green king prawns, peeled (tails intact), deveined
1 tbs lime juice
2 tbs fish sauce*
1 spring onion, sliced
Handful of coriander leaves

Place the tamarind concentrate in a bowl and pour over 1/2 cup (125ml) hot water. Set aside for 10 minutes.

Heat the sunflower oil in a large saucepan. Add the palm sugar and garlic and cook, stirring, for 1 minute until fragrant.

Pour in the stock and bring to the boil, then reduce the heat to low. Strain the tamarind liquid into the pan and add the lemongrass, galangal, lime leaves and chilli. Simmer the soup for 15 minutes or until the aromatics have infused the stock.

Add the prawns and simmer for 2-3 minutes or until they are pink and just cooked. Stir in the lime juice, fish sauce, spring onion and coriander, then ladle into serving bowls.

* Tamarind concentrate, palm sugar, galangal, kaffir lime leaves and fish sauce are all available from Asian food shops. Fish stock is available from selected delis and fishmongers. **d.**

Blue cheese, onion & pine nut focaccia

starters

23 warm pumpkin & goat's cheese salad
23 blue cheese, onion & pine nut focaccia
23 mulled pear salad with roquefort dressing
24 duck rillettes
24 winter ceviche of kingfish and salmon
27 mini tapas
27 vodka-cured salmon with watercress pancakes

Mulled pear salad with roquefort dressing

Warm pumpkin & goat's cheese salad

starters.

warm pumpkin & goat's cheese salad
Serves 4

½ small jap pumpkin (skin on),
   cut into thin wedges
100ml olive oil
1 tbs thyme leaves
150g firm goat's cheese,
   cut into rounds
1 cup panko breadcrumbs*
2 tbs balsamic vinegar
1 tsp Dijon mustard
4 cups baby salad leaves (mesclun)

Preheat the oven to 200°C.
   Toss pumpkin with 2 tablespoons of the oil and thyme. Season with salt and freshly ground black pepper. Place on a baking tray and roast for 30 minutes, turning once, until cooked and lightly caramelised. Set aside to cool slightly.
   Meanwhile, brush the goat's cheese rounds with 1 tablespoon of remaining olive oil and coat in the breadcrumbs. Place on a separate greased baking tray and chill in the fridge until just before you're ready to serve the salad.
   Whisk together the vinegar, mustard and remaining 2 tablespoons of oil. Season to taste with salt and pepper.
   Place the goat's cheese in the oven for 5-6 minutes until crumbs are golden.
   Toss the salad leaves and pumpkin in half the vinaigrette and pile onto plates. Add the warmed goat's cheese and drizzle with the remaining vinaigrette.
* From Asian food shops. Substitute dry breadcrumbs.

blue cheese, onion & pine nut focaccia
Serves 6

1¾ cups (260g) strong (baker's) flour*
1 tsp dry active yeast (about ½ sachet)*
1 tsp honey
2 tbs olive oil
40g unsalted butter, softened
100g strong blue cheese (such as
   gorgonzola, Stilton or Roquefort)
2 tbs toasted pine nuts
½ small red onion, thinly sliced

Stir ⅓ cup (50g) flour in a bowl with yeast, honey and ½ cup (125ml) lukewarm water. Stand for 20 minutes until starting to froth.
   Place remaining 210g flour in a large bowl. Make a well in centre, then add yeast mixture, oil and 1 tsp salt. Mix with your hands to form a soft but firm dough, then turn out onto a floured surface and knead for 10 minutes or until smooth, elastic and shiny. (Or knead using dough hook of an electric mixer.) Transfer to a clean, lightly oiled bowl, cover with a tea towel and leave to rise in a warm place for 1 hour or until doubled in size.
   Preheat oven to 200°C and lightly oil 2 baking trays. Punch the dough with your fist to knock out the air, then divide into 2. Roll each into a 2cm-thick, 25cm x 30cm rectangle, then place on trays.
   In a small bowl, mash butter and cheese together with a fork, then fold in the nuts. Spread half the mixture lengthways down 1 half of each focaccia, leaving a 1cm border around the edges. Brush borders with water, then fold over to make 2 long rectangles, pressing down edges gently. Score a couple of shallow slashes in top. Scatter focaccias with most of the onion, reserving a little to garnish. Bake for 8–10 minutes until pale golden. Cut into wedges, then serve warm, garnished with remaining onion.
* From the baking aisle in supermarkets.

mulled pear salad with roquefort dressing
Serves 6

1 tbs cabernet* or red wine vinegar
¼ cup (60ml) walnut oil*
150ml creme fraiche
200g strong blue cheese (such as
   Roquefort*)
4 cups baby salad leaves (mesclun)
1 cup (100g) toasted walnuts, chopped

Mulled pears
6 small pears (not too ripe), halved, cored
300ml fruity red wine (we used merlot)
⅓ cup (75g) caster sugar
1 vanilla bean, split, seeds scraped
1 cinnamon quill
2 whole cloves

For mulled pears, place pears in a pan that fits them snugly. Pour over wine, sugar, vanilla pod and seeds, spices and 300ml water, then cover surface closely with a sheet of baking paper. Bring to a simmer over medium-high heat, then cook for 10-15 minutes until tender (this will depend on the ripeness of the pears). Remove pears, then simmer liquid until reduced by half. Pour over pears and allow to steep in liquid until ready to serve (up to 24 hours).
   Whisk the cabernet, oil and 2-3 tbs poaching liquid in a bowl. Season, then set the vinaigrette aside. For the Roquefort dressing, warm the creme fraiche and half the Roquefort in a small pan over low heat for 2-3 minutes, stirring until smooth.
   Toss leaves and walnuts with vinaigrette, then divide among plates. Top with pears, crumble over remaining cheese, then serve warm Roquefort dressing in small jugs or shot glasses to pour at the table.
* From gourmet food shops and delis.

starters.

Duck rillettes

duck rillettes
Serves 6-8

4 duck legs and 2 duck breasts*
6 whole black peppercorns, plus extra to garnish
6 juniper berries*
1 piece blade mace*
3 garlic cloves, sliced
3 thyme sprigs
2 fresh bay leaves, plus extra to garnish
1 cup (250ml) dry white wine
Cold toasts and relishes, to serve

Preheat the oven to 150°C.

Place the duck legs and breasts in a single layer, skin-side up, in a roasting pan. Lightly crush the peppercorns, juniper berries and mace in a pestle and mortar and scatter around the duck. Add the garlic, thyme sprigs, bay leaves and wine. Season with sea salt, cover tightly with foil and cook for 2 hours 30 minutes until the meat falls off the bone.

Tip the contents of the roasting pan into a colander set over a bowl. When cool enough to handle, remove and discard the skin and bones and shred the meat. Moisten the meat with a little of the strained fat, season and pack into a 1.4L terrine or loaf pan.

Leave mixture to cool and spoon over a little fat. Decorate with extra peppercorns and bay leaves and chill for 2-3 days until ready to serve. Serve with cold toasts and relishes.
* Duck can be ordered from poultry shops and butchers. Dried juniper berries are from supermarkets and delis. Blade mace is from spice shops.

winter ceviche of kingfish and salmon
Serves 6

¼ cup (60ml) freshly squeezed orange juice
2 tbs lime juice
2 tbs olive oil
2 tsp sesame oil
1 tbs fish sauce
300g each sashimi-grade* kingfish and salmon fillet, thinly sliced
1 long red chilli, seeds removed, finely chopped
1 tbs roughly torn coriander leaves
1 tbs small mint leaves
1 small red onion, very thinly sliced
2 tbs pomegranate seeds* (optional, or use 1 orange or pink grapefruit segment, broken into small pieces)

Whisk the orange and lime juice in a bowl with oils and fish sauce.

Alternate the kingfish and salmon slices on 6 serving plates. Scatter with the chopped chilli, coriander, mint, onion and pomegranate or citrus.

Drizzle with the dressing just before serving.
* Order sashimi-grade fish from fishmongers. Fresh pomegranates are available in season from greengrocers.

Winter ceviche of kingfish and salmon

Mini tapas

starters.

Vodka-cured salmon with watercress pancakes

mini tapas
Serves 4
Pop in to your local deli and choose a mixture of marinated vegetables, cheeses and cold meats. We've used pan-fried chorizo with parsley and garlic, jamon* or prosciutto slices, manchego* cheese, quince paste and marinated olives. Serve with this easy broad bean salad and classic tomato-rubbed bread.

1 cup frozen broad beans (or we used canned mini broad beans*)
4 roast capsicum pieces (about 180g total), cut into strips
1½ tbs extra virgin olive oil

Tomato-rubbed bread (pan con tomate)
4 slices sourdough bread
1-2 tbs extra virgin olive oil
1 garlic clove, halved
2 tomatoes, halved

Blanch frozen broad beans in boiling salted water for 2-3 minutes. Drain and refresh, then peel. (For canned baby beans, just drain.) Toss the broad beans, capsicum and oil in a bowl, season, then transfer to a serving dish.

For tomato-rubbed bread, brush sourdough with oil and grill 1-2 minutes each side until golden. While warm, rub with cut side of garlic, then cut side of tomato, allowing juice to soak into bread.
* From delis and gourmet shops.

vodka-cured salmon with watercress pancakes
Serves 4-6 as a starter
Start the salmon a day ahead.

200g skinless salmon fillet, pin-boned
2 tsp caster sugar
2 tbs chopped dill, plus sprigs to serve
¼ cup (60ml) vodka
1 small beetroot, cooked, peeled (to give about 80g beetroot)

Vodka creme fraiche
30ml vodka
½ cup (120g) creme fraiche
1 tbs lemon juice

Watercress pancakes
¾ cup (110g) plain flour
½ tsp bicarbonate of soda
1 tsp cream of tartar
1 egg
2 cups picked watercress leaves (you need about ½ a bunch)
150ml milk
Melted unsalted butter, to grease

Rinse the salmon and dry well with paper towel. Mix the sugar and dill in a dish with 1 tbs sea salt. Add salmon and turn to coat. Pour over vodka, cover with plastic wrap and chill for 4 hours, turning twice. Grate beetroot into dish and turn salmon to coat. Chill for a further 6 hours, turning occasionally.

Wipe the salmon clean using paper towel, then cut into 1cm cubes. Cover and refrigerate until ready to serve.

Combine creme fraiche ingredients in a bowl and refrigerate until ready to serve.

For the pancakes, preheat oven to 150°C. Place flour, bicarbonate of soda, cream of tartar, egg and watercress in a food processor. Process slowly, gradually adding milk, until a smooth batter forms.

Working in batches, brush a non-stick frypan with butter, and place over medium-high heat. Drop 2 tsp of batter in pan for each pancake, spacing pancakes 2-3cm apart. Cook for 1-2 minutes until bubbles appear on surface, then turn and cook for a further minute or until golden. Transfer to a baking tray, cover loosely with foil and keep warm in oven, greasing pan with butter as needed.

Place salmon in a serving bowl and garnish with dill sprigs. Set out with the pancakes and vodka creme fraiche. **d.**

Prawn, watercress & salmon pie

pies

- **31** satay pork pies
- **31** prawn, watercress & salmon pie
- **31** chicken korma pies
- **32** sausage pasty
- **32** lamb & rosemary hotpots
- **35** spiced kumara pies with yoghurt pastry
- **35** creamy chicken, leek & bacon pie
- **36** beef wellington pie
- **36** butternut, spinach & goat's cheese pie
- **39** beef, stout & potato pies
- **39** chicken, mushroom & taleggio torta

Chicken korma pies

Satay pork pies

pies.

satay pork pies
Makes 6

1 onion, chopped
2 garlic cloves, chopped
2 tsp grated ginger
1 tbs crunchy peanut butter
3 tbs chopped unsalted peanuts
1 tbs sweet chilli sauce, plus extra to serve
1 tbs soy sauce
2 tbs peanut oil
200g pork mince
1/4 cup (35g) plain flour
1 carrot, coarsely grated
1 cup (250ml) chicken stock
1/4 cup (60ml) coconut cream
2 tbs chopped coriander leaves
6 frozen puff pastry sheets, thawed
1 egg, beaten
Salad, to serve

Place the onion, garlic, ginger, peanut butter, peanuts, sweet chilli sauce and soy sauce in a food processor and pulse to form a coarse paste.

Heat the oil in a deep frypan over medium heat. Add the paste and stir for 2-3 minutes or until fragrant. Add pork and cook, stirring, for 3-4 minutes until browned. Stir in flour, carrot and stock. Bring to the boil, reduce heat to low and simmer for 10 minutes or until mixture thickens. Stir in coconut cream and coriander. Allow to cool slightly.

Preheat the oven to 190°C. Grease six holes of 1/3 cup (80ml) muffin pan. Use pastry cutters to cut out six 10cm rounds and six 5cm rounds from pastry. Use 10cm rounds to line muffin holes. Fill with the pork mixture and top with 5cm rounds, pressing edges to seal. Brush top with egg. Bake for 20 minutes or until golden. Serve with extra sweet chilli sauce and salad.

prawn, watercress & salmon pie
Serves 6

75g unsalted butter
1/2 cup (75g) plain flour, plus extra to dust
600ml full-fat milk
2 bay leaves
1 tsp English mustard
1/2 bunch watercress, sprigs picked, finely chopped
8 large green prawns, peeled, deveined, halved
800g skinless, boneless salmon fillets, cut into 2cm pieces
1 cup (120g) frozen peas
2 frozen shortcrust pastry sheets, thawed
1 egg, beaten

Melt the butter in a saucepan over medium-low heat. Add the flour and stir for 2 minutes until smooth. Add a little milk and stir until smooth. Gradually add the remaining milk, stirring, then add the bay leaves. Gently simmer for 3-5 minutes until thickened. Remove from heat, season and stir in the mustard and watercress.

Scatter the prawns, salmon and frozen peas in a 2L pie dish. Pour over the sauce and leave to cool completely.

Preheat the oven to 200°C.

Cut the pastry sheets into 2cm-wide strips. Brush the rim of the dish with egg, then place half the strips, at intervals, all going in one direction. Cross with the remaining strips to make a lattice, lifting and weaving them in and out of each other (this is fiddly).

Brush the top with beaten egg. Bake for 25 minutes until the pastry is golden brown and the sauce is bubbling.

chicken korma pies
Serves 4

1.5kg whole chicken
2 leeks (white part only), sliced
4 garlic cloves, 2 sliced, 2 crushed
8cm piece ginger, 5cm piece sliced, 3cm piece grated
2 bay leaves
4 frozen shortcrust pastry sheets, thawed
2 frozen puff pastry sheets, thawed
50g unsalted butter
1 onion, finely chopped
3 tbs korma (or other mild) curry paste
1 tsp ground cumin
1/4 tsp cayenne pepper
1/4 cup (35g) plain flour
300ml coconut milk
150g green beans, halved, blanched
1 large parsnip, halved lengthways, sliced on angle, blanched, refreshed
1 cup chopped coriander leaves
1 egg, lightly beaten

Place chicken, leek, sliced garlic and ginger, bay leaves, 1 tbs sea salt and 2.25L water in a pan and bring to the boil. Reduce heat to low and simmer, covered, for 45 minutes until chicken is cooked, then transfer to a plate, reserving stock.

Grease four 11cm pie dishes. Cut four 17cm rounds of shortcrust pastry and four 11cm rounds of puff pastry. Use shortcrust rounds to line dishes and chill, along with puff pastry rounds.

Strain stock into a bowl, discarding vegetables, then return to the pan. Boil over high heat for 15-20 minutes until reduced by about two-thirds. Set aside.

Melt butter in a large pan over medium-low heat. Add onion and cook, stirring, for 6-8 minutes until soft. Add crushed garlic, grated ginger, paste, cumin and cayenne pepper and cook, stirring, for 1-2 minutes until fragrant. Stir in flour and cook for 1 minute, then gradually whisk in stock and coconut milk. Increase heat to medium and bring to the boil, stirring, then set aside.

Remove chicken skin and bones and shred meat. Stir into sauce with beans, parsnip and coriander. Season. Transfer to a large shallow dish and chill for 20-30 minutes to cool completely.

Spoon mixture into dishes. Place puff rounds on top and press edges to seal. Brush with egg. Chill for 30 minutes.

Preheat oven to 200°C. Bake pies for 20-25 minutes until pastry is crisp and golden and filling is bubbling hot.

pies.

Sausage pasty

lamb & rosemary hotpots
Serves 4

To make this as a large hotpot, use a large, shallow ovenproof dish. Bake, covered with foil, for 30 minutes, then remove the foil and bake for a further 20 minutes.

1 tbs olive oil
1kg lamb neck fillets, cut into 1-2cm pieces
1 large onion, sliced
500g carrots, thickly sliced
2 garlic cloves, finely chopped
2 tbs plain flour
2 cups (500ml) lamb or beef stock, hot
1 tbs Worcestershire sauce, or to taste
1 tbs finely chopped rosemary leaves, plus extra to sprinkle
400g King Edward or pontiac potatoes, thinly sliced
30g unsalted butter, chopped

Preheat the oven to 190°C. Heat the oil in a large, heavy-based casserole. Season the lamb and cook, in batches, over high heat until golden brown. Remove with a slotted spoon. Set aside.

Reduce the heat to medium, add the onion and carrot and cook for 5 minutes. Add the garlic and fry for a further 1 minute. Stir in the flour and cook for 1 minute, then return the lamb to the pan with stock, Worcestershire sauce and rosemary. Season and bring to the boil. Cover with a lid, reduce the heat to low and simmer for 30 minutes until the lamb is tender.

Preheat the oven to 200°C.

Divide the lamb mixture between four 18cm, 2-cup (500ml) pie dishes, cover with the potato and dot with butter. Sprinkle with extra rosemary. Season well. Cover dishes with foil and bake for 20 minutes, then remove the foil and bake for a further 25 minutes until bubbling and golden brown.

sausage pasty
Serves 4-6

700g good-quality sausages
1 tbs olive oil
1 large onion, chopped
2 garlic cloves, chopped
1 tbs tomato paste
1 cup (260g) tomato passata (sugo)*
1 tbs chopped flat-leaf parsley
375g block frozen puff pastry, thawed
Plain flour, to dust
1 egg, beaten
Good-quality chilli sauce, to serve

Remove sausage meat from casings and discard casings. Heat oil in a saucepan over medium-low heat, add onion and garlic and cook, stirring, for 5 minutes or until onion has softened. Increase heat to high and add sausage meat, then cook, stirring with a wooden spoon to break up. When meat is starting to brown, stir in tomato paste, passata and 1/3 cup (80ml) water, then cook for a further 5 minutes. Set aside to cool. Place mixture in a food processor with parsley and pulse until just combined. Season to taste.

Preheat oven to 180°C. Line a baking tray with baking paper.

Cut pastry in half lengthways. Roll out one piece on a lightly floured surface to a 18cm x 35cm rectangle. Place on the tray and top with sausage mixture, leaving a 2cm border. Brush the border with water. Roll out remaining pastry on a lightly floured surface so that it is slightly larger than the first rectangle. Make several small slashes across middle of the pastry. Place over the sausage meat and seal edges. Brush the pastry with beaten egg and bake for 25 minutes until puffed and golden. Serve with chilli sauce.

* Sieved tomatoes, from supermarkets.

Lamb & rosemary hotpots

Spiced kumara pies with yoghurt pastry

pies.

spiced kumara pies with yoghurt pastry
Makes 10

2 tbs sunflower oil
1 onion, finely chopped
1 garlic clove, crushed
1 tsp good-quality mild curry powder
1 medium (about 200g) kumara, peeled, cut into 2cm pieces
1/3 cup (80ml) vegetable stock
Zest of 1 orange, plus juice of 1/2 orange
2-3 tbs chopped coriander leaves
1 egg, beaten
Thick Greek yoghurt mixed with chopped coriander, and wild rocket, to serve

Yoghurt pastry
280g plain flour, plus extra to dust
200g chilled unsalted butter, chopped
1 cup (280g) thick Greek yoghurt

For yoghurt pastry, place flour, butter and a pinch of salt in a food processor and whiz until the mixture resembles fine breadcrumbs. Add yoghurt and process until the mixture comes together. Knead lightly to form a dough, dusting with more flour if needed. Divide into 2 equal pieces and enclose each in plastic wrap. Chill for 30-60 minutes or until firm. Dust pastry with flour and roll between 2 sheets of baking paper, dusting with more flour if overly sticky, until 2-3mm thick. Chill.

Heat oil in a saucepan over medium-low heat. Cook onion for 5 minutes until soft. Stir in garlic, curry powder and kumara. Add stock, zest and juice and season. Reduce heat to low, cover and bring to a simmer. Cook for 10 minutes until kumara is cooked through. Remove from the heat and mash until smooth. Stir in coriander and season. Cool.

Preheat the oven to 190°C. Use a 10cm pastry cutter to cut out 20 rounds. Place heaped 1 tbs filling on 10 pastry rounds. Brush edges with egg. Top with remaining rounds. Press edges to seal. Brush tops with egg. Cut 2-3 slits on top of each pie. Bake for 20-25 minutes until golden. Cool slightly. Serve with yoghurt and rocket.

Creamy chicken & leek pie

creamy chicken, leek & bacon pie
Serves 4

1.2kg whole chicken
1 each carrot and onion, chopped
1 bouquet garni*
1 tbs olive oil
1 leek, thickly sliced
100g bacon rashers, cut into strips
50g unsalted butter
1/3 cup (50g) plain flour, plus extra to dust
100g creme fraiche or sour cream
1 tbs grainy mustard
375g frozen block puff pastry, thawed
1 egg, beaten
Peas, to serve

Place chicken in a large heavy-based pan over high heat. Add carrot, onion and bouquet garni and cold water to cover, then bring to boil. Simmer, uncovered, over medium-low heat for 45 minutes. Remove chicken and shred meat into bite-sized pieces. Return the bones to the pan of stock and simmer over medium-high heat for 30 minutes until reduced to 600ml. Strain and discard solids.

Heat the oil in a large pan over medium heat. Cook the leek and bacon, stirring, for 2-3 minutes until the leek softens and the bacon starts to crisp. Add the butter, and when melted, add the flour and stir for 1 minute. Add the stock and cook for a further 3-4 minutes. Stir in the creme fraiche, mustard and chicken. Set aside to cool completely.

Preheat the oven to 200°C. Spoon the mixture into a 1L rectangular pie dish. Roll out the pastry on a lightly floured surface until 5mm thick. Cut a 1cm-wide strip and press around dish rim to make a 'collar'. Brush with egg. Place remaining pastry over, press edges and trim. Cut an air vent. Brush pie top with egg. Bake for 20-25 minutes until golden brown.

* Tie 2 fresh bay leaves and 2 sprigs each thyme and parsley with kitchen string.

pies.

Beef Wellington pie

beef wellington pie
Serves 6

1 tbs sunflower oil
900g chuck steak, cut into 5cm pieces
3 tbs plain flour, plus extra to dust
800ml beef stock, hot
4 thyme sprigs
30g unsalted butter
2 small eschalots, finely chopped
2 garlic cloves, finely chopped
250g Swiss brown mushrooms, sliced
12 slices (about 135g) prosciutto, chopped
15g dried porcini mushrooms*, soaked in 100ml boiling water
¼ cup (60ml) brandy or cognac
375g block frozen puff pastry, thawed
1 egg, beaten

Heat the oil in a large heavy-based frypan. Season the beef, then cook, in batches, over high heat until browned all over, then transfer to a plate. Return all the beef to pan, add the flour and stir to coat. Add the stock and 2 thyme sprigs, then bring to a simmer. Reduce heat to low, then cover and cook for 2 hours 30 minutes until beef is tender.

Meanwhile, melt butter in a frypan over medium-low heat. Add eschalot, garlic and remaining thyme, leaves picked, and cook until softened. Add Swiss brown mushrooms and prosciutto, increase heat to high and cook for 2-3 minutes until there is no moisture left in the pan.

Meanwhile, drain porcini, reserving the soaking liquid, then finely chop and add to the pan. Strain reserved soaking liquid through a sieve lined with paper towel (to remove any grit) and add to pan with the brandy. Cook for 3-4 minutes or until there is no liquid remaining. Season well with black pepper but no salt. Combine with the beef mixture, then spoon into a deep, 1.5L (6-cup) pie dish. Cool completely.

Roll out pastry on a lightly floured surface. Cut a 1cm-wide strip from pastry and press around dish rim to make a 'collar'. Brush with egg, then cover with remaining pastry, press edges and trim. Brush top with egg. Cut an air vent. Chill for 20 minutes.

Preheat the oven to 200°C. Bake for 20-25 minutes until golden brown.

* Dried porcini mushrooms are from gourmet food shops and greengrocers.

butternut, spinach & goat's cheese pie
Serves 8-10

2 (about 1kg each) butternut pumpkins, peeled, seeds removed, sliced 1cm-thick slices
⅓ cup (80ml) olive oil
2 tsp cumin seeds, toasted
2 tsp ras el hanout* or Moroccan seasoning
Pinch of dried chilli flakes
2-3 red onions, thinly sliced
4 garlic cloves, skins on
1kg baby spinach leaves, blanched, chopped
250g fresh ricotta
1 qty cheese pastry (see Basics, p 136)
⅓ cup (50g) pine nuts, toasted
200g soft goat's cheese, crumbled
1 egg, beaten
2 tbs grated parmesan

Preheat oven to 200°C. Place pumpkin on 2-3 large, lined roasting trays. Drizzle with 2 tbs oil, scatter with cumin seeds, ras el hanout and chilli. Season well. Roast for 40 minutes, then scatter with onion and garlic and toss together. Roast vegetables for a further 20 minutes until browned. Squeeze garlic from skin and mash into onion. Leave to cool slightly.

Place spinach in a bowl and season. Add ricotta and combine. Set aside.

Roll out two-thirds of pastry on a lightly floured surface until 2-3mm thick, and use to line the base and sides of a 23cm springform pan. Add half the spinach mixture, then top with half the pumpkin. Press down slightly. Scatter with half the pine nuts, then half the goat's cheese. Repeat with remaining fillings. Finish with a layer of the onion.

Roll out remaining pastry on a lightly floured surface. Place over pie, press edges to seal and cut an air vent. Brush with egg. Chill for 20 minutes.

Preheat oven to 200°C. Sprinkle pie with parmesan and bake for 35-40 minutes until golden brown. Cool in pan for 10 minutes before serving.

* Moroccan spice blend, from Middle Eastern and specialty spice shops.

Butternut, spinach & goat's cheese pie

Beef, stout & potato pies

pies.

beef, stout & potato pies
Makes 6

1kg chuck steak, cut into 3cm pieces
¼ cup (35g) plain flour, seasoned
20g unsalted butter
2 tbs olive oil
2 onions, chopped
2 garlic cloves, finely chopped
2 carrots, finely chopped
1 tbs tomato paste
2 tsp Worcestershire sauce
400ml Guinness or stout
1 bay leaf
1½ cups (375ml) beef stock
6 frozen puff pastry sheets, thawed
1 egg, beaten
Mixed salad leaves, to serve

Lightly coat beef in flour, shaking off and reserving excess flour.
　Heat butter and oil in a large flameproof casserole or saucepan over medium-high heat. Cook beef, in batches, for 3-4 minutes until browned all over, then remove and set aside.
　Add onion, garlic and carrot to the same pan (with a little extra oil if needed) and stir for 2-3 minutes. Return beef to pan, stir in paste and reserved flour, then add sauce, stout, bay leaf, potato and stock. Bring to the boil, then reduce the heat to low. Cover and cook for 1½ hours or until beef is tender and sauce is thick. Cool completely.
　Preheat the oven to 190°C. Cut two 1cm-wide strips from sides of each pastry sheet. Set aside. Cut pie lids from remaining pastry, 1cm wider than the top of six 2-cup (500ml) pie dishes or ovenproof bowls. Divide beef mixture among dishes. Press pastry strips around each rim to make a 'collar' and brush with water. Carefully top with pie lids and press firmly around edges to seal well. Trim edges with a sharp knife. Make 2 cuts in pie tops, then brush with egg. Bake for 25-30 minutes until golden. Serve with steamed potatoes and salad.

Chicken, mushroom & Taleggio torta

chicken, mushroom & taleggio torta
Serves 4

20g unsalted butter
1 tbs olive oil
1 garlic clove, finely chopped
250g Swiss brown mushrooms, sliced
200g baby spinach leaves
1 tbs thyme leaves
4 frozen puff pastry sheets, thawed, plus pastry 'leaves' to decorate
⅔ cup onion marmalade*
2 poached chicken breast fillets, shredded (or 2 cups shredded barbecued chicken)
300g Taleggio cheese*, thinly sliced
1 egg, beaten

Preheat oven to 190°C. Melt butter and oil in a pan over medium heat. Cook garlic and mushrooms, stirring, for 3-4 minutes until mushrooms soften. Increase heat to medium-high. Cook for 2-3 minutes until liquid is almost evaporated. Add spinach and thyme. Season. Cook 1 minute to wilt. Press in a sieve to remove liquid. Cool.
　Lay 1 pastry sheet on a work surface with one corner pointing towards you. Spread with 2 tbs onion, leaving a 4cm border. Top with a quarter of the chicken, then a quarter each of the mushroom mix and cheese. Brush edges with egg, then bring all 4 corners up to form a parcel and press edges together to seal. Place on a large lined baking tray. Repeat to make 4 tortas. Decorate with pastry leaves, then brush with egg and bake for 20 minutes or until golden and puffed.
* Onion marmalade and Taleggio (a soft, Italian washed-rind cheese) are from delis and gourmet shops. **d.**

Chickpeas with winter vegetables and saffron

braises

43 lamb paprikash
43 chickpeas with winter vegetables and saffron
43 traditional beef daube
44 pork goulash with paprika yoghurt
44 braised veal shanks with sicilian olives and gremolata
47 chicken tagine with preserved lemon
47 sausage & lentil braise
48 slow-cooked lamb with parsley dumplings
48 duck breast ragu with soft polenta

Traditional beef daube

Lamb paprikash

braises.

lamb paprikash
Serves 6

30g unsalted butter
2 tbs olive oil
6 French-trimmed lamb shanks
2 onions, chopped
1 tsp caraway seeds
1½ tbs paprika
4 garlic cloves, finely chopped
2 bay leaves
2 red capsicums, thinly sliced
1 tbs tomato paste
400g can chopped tomatoes
1½ cups (375ml) beef stock
1 cup (250ml) red wine
1½ tbs red wine vinegar
2 large potatoes, cut into 2cm cubes
2 tbs chopped flat-leaf parsley leaves
Sour cream, to serve

Noodle kugels
150g spaghettini
100g sour cream
1 egg, lightly beaten
1 onion, grated
1 garlic clove, finely chopped
2 tbs chopped flat-leaf parsley leaves

Preheat the oven to 170°C.

Melt half the butter with 1 tbs oil in a large flameproof casserole over medium heat. In 2 batches, brown the lamb on all sides to seal. Remove the shanks from the pan and set aside.

Heat remaining butter and oil in the pan over medium heat, add the onion and cook for 10 minutes or until softened. Add spices, garlic and bay leaves and cook, stirring, for a further minute. Return lamb to pan with capsicum, tomato paste, tomatoes, stock, wine and vinegar, then bring to the boil, skimming the surface. Cover and bake for 1 hour 30 minutes. Add the potato, cover and bake for a further 30 minutes or until potato is tender and the meat is almost falling off the bone.

Meanwhile, for kugels, grease six 8cm-wide, 4cm-deep baking rings or ½ cup (125ml) ramekins. Place on a tray.

Cook pasta to packet instructions. Drain and rinse in cold water, then drain again. Place in a bowl with remaining ingredients, then season and stir to combine. Divide mixture among ramekins and bake during final 20 minutes of paprikash cooking time, until tops start to crisp and turn golden. Run a knife around the inside of the moulds and turn out.

Serve the lamb paprikash drizzled with sour cream and sprinkled with parsley, with noodle kugels on the side.

chickpeas with winter vegetables and saffron
Serves 6

3 carrots, cut into 3cm pieces
2 parsnips, cut into 3cm pieces
350g King Edward potatoes, roughly chopped
Pinch of saffron threads
300ml vegetable stock, heated
2 tbs olive oil
2 garlic cloves, sliced
2cm piece ginger, sliced
2 red onions, sliced
½ tsp dried mint
½ tsp crushed chillies (optional)
400g can whole roma tomatoes
1 fennel bulb, cut into 2cm-thick wedges
400g can chickpeas

Place the carrot, parsnip and potato in a medium saucepan. Pour in enough cold salted water to cover the vegetables. Bring to the boil over high heat, then reduce the heat to medium and simmer for 2-3 minutes until the vegetables are tender. Transfer the vegetables to a plate and set aside. Discard the cooking water.

Meanwhile, soak the saffron in the stock and set aside.

Heat the oil in the same pan over medium heat. Add garlic and ginger and cook, stirring, until just browning. Stir in onion, mint and chilli and cook for 5 minutes until starting to colour.

Add the tomatoes and bring to a simmer. Reduce the heat to medium-low. Add the fennel and chickpeas and their juices. Return the vegetables to the pan. Pour in the stock and simmer, stirring halfway, for 25 minutes until tender. Season to taste, then serve.

traditional beef daube
Serves 6

1 onion, 1 carrot & 1 celery stalk, chopped
2 tsp quatre epices (a mix of pepper, cloves, nutmeg and ginger)
2 garlic cloves, bruised
2 bay leaves
¼ cup (60ml) brandy
1.5L (6 cups) dry red wine
1kg chuck steak, cut into 3cm cubes
¼ cup (60ml) olive oil
60g unsalted butter
1½ tbs tomato paste
2 tbs plain flour
400ml beef stock
250g pancetta or speck, cut into strips
150g button mushrooms
12 eschalots, simmered for 8-10 minutes in water with 2 tsp sugar
Potato mash, to serve

Place onion, carrot, celery, spice, garlic, bay, brandy, wine and beef in a bowl. Cover and marinate in the fridge for at least 4 hours, preferably overnight.

Preheat oven to 170°C. Strain mixture, reserving marinade, beef and vegetables separately. Boil marinade over medium-high heat for 6 minutes, skimming.

Heat 1½ tbs oil and 30g butter in a large flameproof casserole over medium-high heat. Brown beef in batches. Set aside. Add reserved vegetables and cook, stirring, for 2-3 minutes. Add paste, stir for 1 minute, then stir in flour. Return beef to pan with marinade and stock. Bring to the boil, then cover and cook in the oven for 1 hour 30 minutes.

Heat the remaining butter and oil in a pan over medium heat. Cook the pancetta, stirring, for 2-3 minutes until beginning to crisp, then remove and set aside. Add mushrooms and cook for 2-3 minutes until softened. Set aside.

Skim fat from surface of casserole. Strain, reserving beef and vegetables and returning liquid to pan. Simmer liquid on medium-high heat for 3-4 minutes until reduced and thickened. Return the beef to the sauce with the eschalots, pancetta and mushrooms, then heat through for 5 minutes. Serve with potato mash.

braises.

Pork goulash with paprika yoghurt

braised veal shanks with sicilian olives and gremolata
Serves 4

You can serve this with risotto Milanese (saffron risotto) or on creamy polenta.

40g unsalted butter
2 onions, thinly sliced
1 tbs olive oil
4 veal shanks*
1 cinnamon quill
½ tsp ground allspice
2 tbs marjoram leaves
1 bay leaf
1 cup (250ml) dry white wine
Finely grated zest of 1 lemon
3 cups (750ml) chicken stock
½ cup Sicilian green olives* or other large green olives

Gremolata
1 garlic clove, crushed
½ cup chopped flat-leaf parsley leaves
Finely grated zest of 2 lemons

Preheat the oven to 160°C.
 Melt the butter in a large flameproof casserole over medium heat. Add the sliced onion and cook, stirring, for 3-4 minutes until softened. Remove from the pan and set aside.
 Add the oil to the pan and cook the veal shanks, in batches if necessary, for about 5 minutes, turning, until browned all over. Return the onion to the pan and add the cinnamon, allspice, marjoram, bay leaf, white wine and lemon zest. Add the chicken stock, bring to the boil, then cover and cook in the oven for 2½ hours. Add the Sicilian olives, then cover and cook for a further 30 minutes or until the veal is tender and the meat is almost falling off the bone.
 Meanwhile, for the gremolata, combine the garlic, parsley and lemon zest in a bowl, then set aside.
 Serve braised veal with gremolata.
* Veal shanks are from butchers. Sicilian green olives are from delis.

pork goulash with paprika yoghurt
Serves 4

650g diced pork shoulder
1 tbs olive oil
1 onion, chopped
1 garlic clove, chopped
1 tbs tomato paste
1½ tsp paprika, plus extra to sprinkle
1½ tsp caraway seeds
400g can chopped tomatoes
500g chat potatoes, quartered
1 cup (250ml) beef stock
Handful chopped flat-leaf parsley leaves
¼ cup (70g) natural yoghurt, plus extra to serve

Preheat oven to 160°C. Season the pork. Heat oil in a frypan over medium-high heat. Cook pork for 2-3 minutes until browned all over. Remove and set aside.
 Add onion and cook for 3-4 minutes until very soft. Add garlic and cook for a further minute. Add tomato paste, paprika and caraway seeds and cook, stirring, for 1 minute until fragrant. Add tomatoes, potato and stock. Bring to the boil, then cover with a lid and bake in the oven for 1 hour until the pork and potatoes are tender and the sauce has thickened. Season. Cool slightly. Stir in parsley and yoghurt. Ladle into bowls, top with a dollop of yoghurt and sprinkle with paprika. Serve with bread, if desired.

Braised veal shanks with Sicilian olives and gremolata

Chicken tagine with preserved lemon

braises.

chicken tagine with preserved lemon
Serves 4-6

2 tbs olive oil
8 chicken thighs on the bone, seasoned
2 red onions, sliced into wedges
2 large garlic cloves, finely sliced
1 tbs ras el hanout* or Moroccan seasoning
1 cinnamon quill
1 tsp ground cumin
400g can chopped tomatoes
1 1/2 cups (375ml) chicken stock, heated
2 preserved lemon quarters*, skin finely sliced, flesh and white pith discarded
1 tbs mango chutney
1 1/3 cups (200g) soft dried apricots
Handful blanched almonds
400g can chickpeas, rinsed, drained
Coriander leaves, to garnish
Couscous, to serve

Heat the oil in a flameproof casserole over medium-high heat. Add the chicken and brown all over, then transfer to a bowl. Drain all but 1 tbs oil from the casserole. Reduce the heat to medium, add onion and garlic and cook for 10 minutes until softened.

Stir in the spices, increase the heat to medium and cook, stirring, for a further 1-2 minutes until fragrant.

Return the chicken to the casserole with the tomatoes and stock. Stir through the preserved lemon, chutney, apricots and almonds. Season. Bring to the boil, then reduce the heat to low and simmer for 20-25 minutes or until the thighs are cooked and the sauce is well reduced and sticky. Add chickpeas for the final 5 minutes. Garnish with coriander and serve with couscous.

* Ras el hanout is a blend of powdered Moroccan spices, from Middle Eastern and specialty spice shops. Preserved lemons are from gourmet food shops.

Sausage & lentil braise

sausage & lentil braise
Serves 4

1 small bunch baby (Dutch) carrots, peeled
2 thin parsnips, peeled, quartered lengthways
2 tbs olive oil
3 tsp chopped thyme leaves
8 pork or beef chipolata sausages
2 onions, thinly sliced
2 garlic cloves, crushed
1 tbs brown sugar
1 tbs balsamic vinegar
1 cup (250ml) beef consomme* or stock
400g can brown lentils, rinsed, drained
2 tbs chopped flat-leaf parsley leaves

Preheat the oven to 180°C. Toss the carrots and parsnips in 1 tbs oil, then place in a single layer on a baking tray. Season and sprinkle with 1 tsp of the thyme leaves. Roast, turning once, for 25 minutes until tender and golden.

Meanwhile, heat 1 tbs oil in a large frypan. Cook the sausages, turning, until golden, then set aside.

Drain all but 1 tbs oil from pan and place over medium-low heat. Add onion, season and cook, stirring occasionally, for 20 minutes until soft and golden. Add garlic, sugar, balsamic and remaining 2 tsp thyme and cook, stirring, for a further 2-3 minutes until starting to caramelise. Stir in stock and lentils. Return sausages to pan with the vegetables. Reduce heat to low and gently simmer for 5-6 minutes. Scatter with chopped parsley.

* Beef consomme is available from supermarkets (in tetra packs).

braises.

Slow-cooked lamb with parsley dumplings

slow-cooked lamb with parsley dumplings
Serves 4-6

1kg lamb neck fillets*, trimmed
2 cups (500ml) veal stock*
3 cups (750ml) chicken stock
2 carrots, roughly chopped
1 leek (white part only), chopped
1 celery stalk, roughly chopped
2 garlic cloves, bruised
1 bay leaf
¼ tsp coriander seeds
¼ tsp fennel seeds
¼ tsp whole black peppercorns
1 tbs olive oil
1 eschalot, finely chopped
2 tbs dry sherry
200g Jerusalem artichokes*, peeled, cut into 1cm cubes
½ bunch baby (Dutch) carrots, sliced

Parsley dumplings
1 rosemary sprig
½ cup (55g) powdered suet mix*
1 cup (150g) self-raising flour
½ cup roughly chopped parsley leaves, plus extra leaves to garnish
1 garlic clove, crushed
2 tsp extra virgin olive oil
1 egg yolk
¼ cup (60ml) milk

Place lamb in a large pan. Add veal stock, 1 cup (250ml) chicken stock and enough water to cover lamb. Bring to the boil, skimming surface, then add carrot, leek, celery, garlic, bay leaf and spices. Cover, reduce the heat to medium-low and cook for 2 hours or until the lamb is tender.

About 20 minutes before lamb is ready, make the dumplings. Place remaining 2 cups (500ml) stock in a pan with rosemary sprig and enough water to fill halfway. Bring to the boil. Meanwhile, combine all the remaining ingredients, except milk, in a bowl. Season. Mix with your hands. Gradually mix in enough milk to form a dough. Roll into 12 dumplings, then drop into simmering stock, cover and cook over medium heat for 15-20 minutes until doubled in size and cooked.

When lamb is cooked, strain, reserving 2 cups (500ml) of cooking liquid. Return lamb and liquid to pan. Keep warm.

Heat oil in a pan over medium heat. Add eschalot and cook for 3 minutes until softened. Add sherry and cook until evaporated. Add reserved liquid and cook for 10 minutes or until reduced by half, then add artichoke and carrot. Cook for 8-10 minutes until tender.

Slice lamb and divide among plates. Ladle over vegetables and sauce. Top with dumplings and garnish with parsley.
* Lamb neck fillets and veal stock are from butchers. Jerusalem artichokes are from selected greengrocers. Powdered suet mix is from supermarkets.

duck breast ragu with soft polenta
Serves 4

20g unsalted butter
2 tbs olive oil
2 duck breasts*, trimmed of excess fat, thinly sliced into strips
6 slices pancetta, chopped
1 onion, finely chopped
2 garlic cloves, chopped
1 carrot, finely chopped
1 celery stalk, finely chopped
2 bay leaves
2 tbs tomato paste
1 cup (250ml) dry red wine
600g roasted tomato sugo (see Basics, p 136) or good-quality tomato pasta sauce
1 cup (250ml) chicken stock
Soft polenta and grated parmesan, to serve

Heat butter and oil in a large, deep frypan over medium-high heat. Cook duck until browned. Place duck in a bowl.

Drain all but 1 tbs oil from pan and heat over medium heat. Add pancetta, onion, garlic, carrot, celery and bay leaves and cook, stirring, for 2-3 minutes until they start to colour.

Return duck to pan with any juices and tomato paste. Cook, stirring, for 1 minute. Add wine and cook for 2-3 minutes until liquid has reduced slightly. Add sugo and stock, bring to a simmer, then reduce heat to low, cover and gently simmer for 45 minutes or until duck is tender and sauce has thickened slightly. Season. Serve with polenta and parmesan.
* From butchers and poultry shops. **d.**

Duck breast ragu with soft polenta

Quince & Roquefort frangipane tart

Cooking with V-ZUG

Winter cooking can be healthy as well as flavoursome using the innovative V-ZUG Combi-Steam XSL oven. Find out how with these sensational recipes from V-ZUG Gourmet Academy chef Felix Halter.

The V-ZUG Combi-Steam XSL uses innovative pressure-free steam technology to deliver precise temperature control and retain vitamins while cooking anything from seafood to roasts and cakes. The BakeOmatic feature automatically cooks your favourite dishes, or use the GourmetSteam setting to whip up dozens of pre-programmed sweet and savoury recipes.
For more information and recipes, visit: vzug.com.au.

delicious. V-ZUG ADVERTISING FEATURE

Steamed prawns with rocket salad

STEAMED BLUE-EYE WITH COCONUT, LIME AND CHILLI

1kg blue-eye fillet
2 tbs peanut oil
1 tbs green curry paste
2 tbs grated fresh ginger
2 garlic cloves, crushed
4 kaffir lime leaves
¼ cup shaved coconut or coconut flakes
1 tbs brown sugar, plus extra
¼ cup (60ml) fish sauce, plus extra
400ml coconut cream
Leaves of ½ bunch basil
1 tbs lime juice

Garnish
1 small red onion, shredded
1 tbs coconut flakes, toasted
1 small red chilli, thinly sliced
Pared rind of 1 lime, cut into thin strips
Handful of coriander leaves

Place the fish in your V-ZUG Combi-Steam SL at 80°C for 9 minutes.

Meanwhile, heat oil in a pan over medium heat and stir in curry paste, ginger, garlic, lime leaves, coconut flakes, sugar, fish sauce and coconut cream. Simmer for 10 minutes. Add basil and lime juice and simmer for a further 2 minutes. Puree in a blender, then pass through a sieve into a bowl, pushing down on solids. Cool slightly. Add extra brown sugar and fish sauce to taste.

To serve, place blue-eye on a platter and pour over coconut sauce. Garnish with onion, coconut flakes, chilli, lime and coriander. **Serves 4**

QUINCE & ROQUEFORT FRANGIPANE TART

600g caster sugar
2 quinces, peeled, cut into wedges
Juice of 1 lemon
125g unsalted butter, softened
1 vanilla bean, split, seeds scraped
2 eggs
1/4 cup (35g) plain flour
1 cup (120g) almond meal
100g Roquefort* or other blue cheese, crumbled

Pastry
1 1/2 cups (225g) plain flour
125g chilled unsalted butter, chopped
1/3 cup (50g) icing sugar
1 tsp lemon zest
Pinch of ground cinnamon
1 egg

Preheat your V-ZUG Combi-Steam XSL oven to 80°C (or a regular oven to its lowest temperature).

Combine 500g sugar and 800ml water in a pan. Bring to the boil, then simmer over medium heat, stirring, to dissolve sugar. Add quinces and juice and return to boil. Cover surface closely with a piece of baking paper. Bake for 4 hours or until quince is soft. Drain. Set aside.

For pastry, whiz flour, butter, sugar, zest and cinnamon in a processor until mixture resembles breadcrumbs. Add egg and 2 tbs chilled water and whiz until dough comes together in a ball. Enclose in plastic wrap. Chill for 15 minutes.

Roll pastry to 3mm thick on a floured surface. Line a 23cm loose-bottomed tart pan with pastry. Chill for 15 minutes.

Line pastry with baking paper and fill with pastry weights. Bake for 10 minutes. Remove paper and weights, then bake for a further 10 minutes or until golden.

Meanwhile, beat butter, vanilla seeds and remaining 100g sugar in an electric mixer until thick and pale. Add eggs, 1 at a time, beating well after each. Stir in flour and almond meal.

Lay quinces and cheese on tart base. Pour over frangipane mixture. Bake for 40 minutes or until golden. **Serves 8.**
* Roquefort is available from delis.

Turkey roulade with chestnuts, prunes and bacon

TURKEY ROULADE WITH CHESTNUTS, PRUNES AND BACON

1kg whole skinless turkey breast fillet
100g unsweetened chestnut puree*
1 egg
3/4 cup (125g) pitted prunes, chopped
100g bacon, chopped, pan-fried until crisp
2/3 cup (50g) fresh breadcrumbs
1 thyme sprig, leaves picked
2 tbs chopped flat-leaf parsley
Steamed vegetables, to serve

Preheat your V-ZUG Combi-Steam XSL oven to Hot Air Humid function at 180°C (or regular oven to 200°C).

Place the turkey, skinned-side down, on a clean work surface. Open the tenderloin so that the breast lies flat. Use a knife to slice from the centre of the breast outwards; don't cut all the way through. Repeat with the opposite side. Open breast out so it lies flat in a rectangular shape. Season with sea salt and freshly ground pepper.

To make stuffing, combine the chestnut puree, egg, prunes, bacon, breadcrumbs, thyme and parsley in a bowl. Spread the stuffing over the turkey, then roll the turkey up to enclose. Secure the roulade at 3cm intervals with kitchen string.

Cook for 40 minutes or until the turkey is golden and cooked through – the core temperature should measure 80°C on a meat thermometer. Leave to rest, loosely covered with foil, for 10 minutes.

Remove the string from the turkey roulade, then thickly slice and serve with steamed vegetables.

* Unsweetened chestnut puree is from gourmet food shops; substitute toasted chopped macadamias. **Serves 6.**

Pheasant & fig terrine

PHEASANT & FIG TERRINE

30g unsalted butter
50g bacon, finely chopped
2 eschalots, chopped
1/2 cup (100g) dried figs, finely chopped, soaked in 1 tbs port
500g skinless pheasant breast meat*, chopped into 2cm pieces
100ml pure (thin) cream
1 thyme sprig, leaves picked
150g sliced prosciutto
Cranberry sauce and crusty bread, to serve

Melt butter in a frypan over medium-high heat. Cook bacon, eschalots, soaked figs and half the chopped pheasant, stirring, for 10 minutes or until pheasant is cooked and golden. Cool.

Whiz cream and remaining pheasant in a food processor until well combined. Transfer to a bowl and stir in fig mixture and thyme. Season.

Line a 1L terrine or loaf pan with plastic wrap. Line with prosciutto slices, overlapping slightly and leaving enough overhanging the sides to cover. Fill with pheasant mixture and cover with prosciutto, then plastic wrap. Steam for 40 minutes if using a terrine mould, or 25 minutes if using a loaf pan, at 90°C in your V-ZUG Combi-Steam XSL oven. (Alternatively, place in a roasting pan and pour enough boiling water to come halfway up the sides of the terrine. Cook for 50 minutes at 110°C in a regular oven). Cool.

Cut a piece of cardboard to fit the top of the terrine. Place on top and weigh down with cans. Chill for at least 6 hours or overnight.

Turn terrine out of the mould. Slice thickly and serve with cranberry sauce and bread. **Serves 8.**

* Order pheasant from butchers and poultry shops.

STEAMED PRAWNS WITH ROCKET SALAD

3 semi-dried tomatoes, chopped
1 tsp olive oil
8 thin slices Turkish bread
1 garlic clove
2 tsp Dijon mustard
1 egg yolk
50ml extra virgin olive oil
50ml avocado oil
Juice of 1 lime
Pinch saffron threads
600g green prawns, peeled (tails intact), deveined
300g rocket leaves
1/3 cup (80g) roasted red capsicum, drained, cut into thin strips
4 radishes, trimmed, sliced
1/3 cup (50g) pistachio kernels, toasted, chopped

Use the hot air function to preheat your V-ZUG Combi-Steam XSL oven (or regular oven) to 170°C. Pound semi-dried tomatoes and olive oil in a mortar and pestle to form a paste. Brush onto bread and bake on a baking paper-lined tray for 20 minutes until crisp.

Crush garlic and mustard in a mortar and pestle. Mix in yolk. Add extra virgin and avocado oils in a steady stream, stirring until a thick mayonnaise. Add lime. Stir in saffron and season.

Place prawns on a steamer tray and steam in your V-ZUG Combi-Steam XSL oven for 5 minutes at 80°C. Alternatively, steam prawns over a saucepan of boiling water for 5 minutes. Arrange rocket, capsicum, radishes, pistachios and prawns on plates. Drizzle salad with aioli and serve with croutons. **Serves 4.**

delicious. V-ZUG ADVERTISING FEATURE

VANILLA SPRING ROLLS WITH MANGO

1 ripe mango, very thinly sliced
2 mint leaves, shredded, plus extra to serve
40g unsalted butter, melted
6 sheets fresh filo pastry*
400ml good-quality vanilla ice cream
Icing sugar, raspberry coulis and sliced fresh fruit (such as raspberries, strawberries and mango), to serve

Combine mango and mint in a bowl and set aside.

Cut 2 filo sheets in half widthways. Place 1 whole filo sheet on a chopping board with the shorter side closest to you, then place 1 filo half on the bottom half of the whole sheet to create a double layer. (Keep remaining filo covered with a damp tea towel while you work.) Brush the filo well with the melted butter.

On the bottom half of the filo, use one-quarter of the mango mixture to cover a 10cm x 10cm area. Place small scoops of ice cream down the centre of the mango horizontally.

Fold in the long sides of the pastry, then carefully roll up, to form a spring roll. Repeat with remaining pastry, mango mixture and ice cream. Place spring rolls in the freezer for at least 2 hours or overnight until firm.

On your V-ZUG Combi-Steam SL or XSL oven, run GourmetSteam recipe G 15 and follow the prompts. (Alternatively, preheat your regular oven to 250°C and bake the spring rolls for 3 minutes or until golden.)

Dust rolls with icing sugar, drizzle with coulis and serve with sliced fruit and mint. **Serves 4.**

* Available from the chilled section in supermarkets.

The Swiss Leader

For more information and recipes, visit: vzug.com.au.

Roast chicken with peas and bacon

weeknights

59 baked lamb & apricot couscous
59 sausages and champ mash with eschalot gravy
59 roast chicken with peas and bacon
60 fondue-style macaroni cheese
60 chickpea & chorizo stew
63 spiced meatball curry
63 prosciutto-wrapped ocean trout with roast kumara
64 mushroom & bacon risotto
64 fillet steak with quick red wine sauce

Sausages and champ mash with eschalot gravy

Baked lamb & apricot couscous

weeknights.

sausages and champ mash with eschalot gravy
Serves 4

1.5kg potatoes (such as pontiac or desiree), peeled, chopped
¼ cup (60ml) thickened cream
2 tbs Dijon mustard
150g unsalted butter
4 spring onions (pale part only), finely chopped
1 tbs olive oil
12 pork chipolata sausages or 8 regular thin pork sausages
8 eschalots (about 200g total), thinly sliced
1 tbs plain flour
½ cup (125ml) red wine
1½ cups (375ml) good-quality beef stock*
Flat-leaf parsley leaves, to garnish

Place the potato in a saucepan of cold salted water, bring to the boil and cook for 12-15 minutes or until tender. Drain, then return to the pan with the cream, 1 tbs mustard and 120g butter. Mash until smooth. Stir in spring onion and season. Cover and keep warm.
  Meanwhile, heat the oil in a large frypan over medium-high heat. Prick the sausages with a skewer. Cook, turning, for 6-8 minutes until cooked through and browned. Transfer to a tray and keep warm in a 160°C oven.
  Drain all but 1 tbs oil from pan and return to medium heat. Cook the eschalot for 5 minutes until soft. Add the flour, stir for 30 seconds, then add the wine and stock. Bring to the boil, then simmer over medium-low heat for 10 minutes until thick. Whisk in remaining 1 tbs mustard and 30g butter until well combined. Serve sausages on mash, pour over gravy and garnish with parsley.
* Available from delis.

baked lamb & apricot couscous
Serves 4

1 large onion, thinly sliced
2 tbs olive oil
500g lamb fillets, sinew trimmed
1 tbs ras el hanout* or Moroccan seasoning
2 cinnamon quills
1¼ cups (250g) couscous
300ml chicken stock or water
⅓ cup (50g) chopped dried apricots
⅓ cup chopped coriander leaves, plus extra leaves to serve
400g can chickpeas, rinsed, drained
Lemon wedges, to serve

Preheat the oven to 180°C. Place the onion in a shallow baking dish, toss with the oil and bake for 10 minutes.
  Meanwhile, cut each lamb fillet into 2cm cubes, then season with sea salt and pepper. Add the lamb, ras el hanout and cinnamon to the dish, toss together, then return to the oven for 20 minutes.
  Remove from the oven, sprinkle the couscous over and add the stock, then stir to combine. Cover with foil and return to the oven for 10 minutes until lamb is tender and couscous is cooked. Stir in the apricot, chopped coriander and chickpeas, then cover loosely with foil and stand for 5 minutes to warm through. Scatter with extra coriander and serve with lemon wedges.
* Ras el hanout is from Middle Eastern and gourmet shops.

roast chicken with peas and bacon
Serves 2

1 tbs vegetable oil
15g unsalted butter
2 chicken breast fillets, with skin (wingbone attached – optional)*
1 onion, finely chopped
4 bacon rashers, rind removed, chopped
1 tbs plain flour
150ml chicken stock
Juice of 1 orange
100g frozen peas, thawed
2 tbs chopped flat-leaf parsley leaves
Parsnip mash, to serve

Preheat the oven to 200°C. Heat the oil and butter in a large frypan over medium heat, add the chicken, skin-side down, and cook for 2-3 minutes until golden. Place the chicken, skin-side up, on a baking tray and roast for 10-15 minutes.
  Meanwhile, return the pan to heat, add the onion and cook for 1 minute. Add the bacon and cook for 2 minutes until onion is golden and bacon is crisp. Add the flour and cook, stirring, for 1 minute. Add the stock and juice and cook, stirring, for 1-2 minutes until the sauce is thickened. Season, add the peas and heat for a further 1 minute, then stir through the parsley. Return the chicken to the pan to coat in the sauce. Serve the chicken on parsnip mash with the remaining sauce.
* From good butchers or poultry shops.

weeknights.

Fondue-style macaroni cheese

fondue-style macaroni cheese
Serves 6-8

400g macaroni
1 tbs olive oil
250g sliced pancetta or bacon, chopped
50g unsalted butter
2½ cups (175g) fresh breadcrumbs
2 tbs chopped flat-leaf parsley leaves
600ml each milk and pure (thin) cream
¼ cup (35g) plain flour
225g fontina cheese*, coarsely grated
300g cheddar, coarsely grated

Preheat the oven to 180°C. Grease a 2L baking dish. Cook pasta in a large pan of boiling salted water according to packet instructions. Drain well and set aside.

Meanwhile, heat the oil in a frypan over medium heat. Add the pancetta and stir for 2-3 minutes until starting to crisp. Add the butter and breadcrumbs and stir for 2-3 minutes until golden. Transfer to a food processor with the parsley and pulse briefly to combine.

Place the milk, cream and flour in a large heatproof bowl. Lightly whisk to combine. Add half of each cheese, then set bowl over a pan of simmering water. Allow cheese to melt, then stir gently to combine – don't overmix. Add the pasta, then stir in the remaining cheese. Season, then transfer to the prepared dish. Sprinkle with the pancetta mixture. Bake for 30 minutes until golden.

* A melting Italian cheese from delis and gourmet shops; substitute gruyere.

chickpea & chorizo stew
Serves 3-4

1 tbs olive oil
250g piece pancetta, cut into 1cm cubes
2 chorizo sausages, sliced
1 red onion, chopped
1 red capsicum, chopped
3 garlic cloves, finely chopped
1½ tsp dried oregano
1 large potato, peeled, cut into 1.5cm cubes, cooked for 2-3 minutes until almost tender
400g can chickpeas, rinsed, drained
½ cup (125ml) dry white wine
600ml tomato passata (sugo)*
½ cup (125ml) chicken stock
1 tbs chopped flat-leaf parsley leaves

Heat oil in a flameproof casserole over medium-high heat. Cook pancetta and chorizo, turning, for 2-3 minutes until starting to crisp. Drain on paper towel.

Drain all but 2 tbs oil from pan. Return the pan to medium heat, add the onion and capsicum and cook, stirring, for 5 minutes or until softened. Return the pancetta and chorizo to the pan with the garlic and oregano. Stir for a further minute, then add the potato, chickpeas, wine, passata and stock. Season, bring to the boil, then reduce heat to low and cook for a further 10 minutes or until the sauce has reduced and thickened. Garnish with parsley.

* Passata is sieved tomatoes, available in bottles from supermarkets.

Chickpea & chorizo stew

Spiced meatball curry

spiced meatball curry
Serves 4

450g beef mince
3 onions, 1 roughly grated,
 2 finely chopped
2.5cm piece ginger, grated
2 garlic cloves, finely chopped
1 tbs ground coriander
½ tsp ground cumin
1-1½ tsp cayenne pepper
Bunch coriander, leaves chopped
 (reserve a few leaves, to garnish)
1 tbs sunflower oil
2 tbs tikka masala curry paste
400g can chopped tomatoes
1½ cups (375ml) vegetable stock
Naan bread, to serve

Place the beef, grated onion, ginger, garlic, coriander, cumin, cayenne pepper and coriander in a large bowl, season, then mix until well combined. Using wet hands, form the mixture into about 30 walnut-sized balls, then chill for 30 minutes.

Preheat the oven to 180°C. Line a baking tray with baking paper. Place the meatballs on tray and season. Bake for 20 minutes until browned and cooked through.

Meanwhile, heat the oil in a large frypan over medium heat. Add the chopped onion and cook for 3-4 minutes or until soft and golden. Add the curry paste and cook for 1 minute, then stir in the tomatoes and stock. Simmer for 10 minutes, then add the baked meatballs and cook for a further 10 minutes until the sauce is slightly thickened.

Scatter with coriander leaves and serve with naan bread.

Prosciutto-wrapped ocean trout with roast kumara

prosciutto-wrapped ocean trout with roast kumara
Serves 4

2 kumara, peeled, cut into
 2cm cubes
1 tbs roughly chopped sage leaves
⅓ cup (80ml) olive oil
4 prosciutto slices
4 x 175g skinless ocean trout fillets,
 pin-boned
¼ cup coriander leaves
2 spring onions, trimmed, chopped
1 garlic clove, finely chopped
Juice of ½ lemon

Preheat the oven to 180°C. Toss the kumara on a baking tray with the sage, 1 tbs oil, salt and pepper. Roast, turning once, for 10-12 minutes.

Meanwhile, wrap a slice of prosciutto around the centre of each fish fillet. Heat 1 tbs oil in a heavy-based frypan over high heat. Cook the ocean trout for 2 minutes each side or until prosciutto is slightly browned and crisped. Place fish on kumara and bake for a further 4-5 minutes until cooked through.

While the fish is cooking, pound the coriander, spring onion, garlic and some salt and pepper with a mortar and pestle (or pulse mixture in a food processor). Stir in lemon juice and remaining 2 tbs oil to form a loose sauce.

Divide the roasted kumara and trout fillets among plates. Serve topped with the coriander sauce.

weeknights.

Mushroom & bacon risotto

mushroom & bacon risotto
Serves 4

1/3 cup (80ml) olive oil
1 onion, finely chopped
4 garlic cloves, finely chopped
400g Swiss brown mushrooms, sliced
5 (about 250g total) bacon rashers, sliced
1¼ cups (275g) arborio rice
1L (4 cups) vegetable or chicken stock, heated
½ bunch flat-leaf parsley, leaves roughly chopped

Heat 2 tbs of the oil in a frypan over low heat. Add the onion and garlic and cook for 5 minutes until onion is soft. Remove from the pan and set aside.

Add the remaining 2 tablespoons of oil to the same pan and increase the heat to high. Add the sliced mushrooms and bacon and cook, stirring occasionally, for 10 minutes until dry and golden.

Return the onion mixture to the pan with the arborio rice and stir until well coated in the mixture. Reduce the heat to medium.

Add hot stock to the pan a ladleful at a time, stirring constantly and allowing the stock to be absorbed before adding the next, until all stock has been used, the rice is cooked and the mixture is thick; this will take about 20 minutes. The rice should be creamy but still retaining some bite.

To serve, season with freshly ground black pepper and garnish with chopped parsley leaves.

fillet steak with quick red wine sauce
Serves 4

2 tbs olive oil
4 x 180g beef fillet steaks, trimmed
2 onions, halved, sliced
2 garlic cloves, crushed
200g small button mushrooms, trimmed
2 tsp tomato paste
2 tsp plain flour
1 cup (250ml) dry red wine
1½ cups (375ml) good-quality beef stock*
Potato mash and watercress, to serve

Preheat the oven to 180°C.

Heat 1 tbs of the oil in a frypan over medium-high heat. Season the steaks and cook for 2 minutes each side. Transfer to a baking tray and cook in the oven for a further 2-3 minutes for rare or 5 minutes for medium.

Meanwhile, heat the remaining 1 tbs of oil in the same pan over medium-low heat. Add the onion and cook for 5 minutes or until softened. Add the garlic and mushrooms and stir for 1-2 minutes. Stir in the paste and flour. Add the wine and stock, then bring to the boil. Reduce the heat to medium and simmer for 5-6 minutes until well reduced. Season with salt and pepper. Remove pan from the heat and return steaks to the pan to just warm through in the sauce. Serve the steaks and sauce with potato mash and watercress.
* Available from delis. **d.**

Fillet steak with quick red wine sauce

Thyme-roasted rib of beef with red wine gravy

roasts

- **69** lemon & bacon spatchcocks with bread sauce
- **69** thyme-roasted rib of beef with red wine gravy
- **69** rack of pork with cider apples
- **70** creamy pot-roast chicken
- **70** greek lamb with crispy potatoes
- **73** roast duck with star anise & orange sauce
- **73** rosemary salt roast lamb with boulangère potatoes

Rack of pork with cider apples

Lemon & bacon spatchcocks with bread sauce

roasts.

lemon & bacon spatchcocks with bread sauce
Serves 4

30g unsalted butter
¼ cup (60ml) olive oil
1 leek, chopped
100g Swiss brown mushrooms, chopped
6 thin pork sausages (about 350g total), skins removed
2 lemons, halved, plus 2 tsp grated zest
1 cup (70g) fresh white breadcrumbs
2 x 500g spatchcocks*, rinsed, dried
4 bacon rashers
2 rosemary sprigs, leaves picked

Bread sauce
1 onion, halved
4 cloves
2 cups (500ml) milk
1 bay leaf, plus extra to garnish
4 garlic cloves
2 cups (140g) fresh white breadcrumbs

Preheat oven to 180°C. Melt butter and 1 tbs oil in a pan over medium-high heat. Add leek and mushrooms and cook until softened. Add sausage meat and zest, season and cook for 5-10 minutes until meat is browned. Remove from heat, fold in crumbs and cool completely. Use mixture to stuff the cavities of spatchcocks, then rub outer skins with remaining 2 tbs oil. Lay 2 bacon rashers in a criss-cross pattern over each spatchcock. Sprinkle with sea salt and place on a baking tray along with lemon halves. Sprinkle with the rosemary. Roast for 45-55 minutes until birds are cooked through (juices run clear when thigh is pierced) and skin is crisp.

Meanwhile, for sauce, stud onion with cloves. Bring milk, onion, bay leaf and garlic to the boil in a pan over medium-low heat. Set aside for 30 minutes. Strain and return milk mixture to pan. Add bread and season with sea salt and freshly ground black pepper. Simmer for 5 minutes until sauce has thickened. Serve sauce with the spatchcocks.
* Baby chickens, from specialty poultry shops and selected supermarkets.

thyme-roasted rib of beef with red wine gravy
Serves 4-6

2.5-3kg forerib of beef (2 ribs), chined*
Olive oil, to rub
2 tsp thyme leaves, plus extra to garnish
1 small red onion, finely sliced
2 tsp plain flour
200ml good-quality red wine
2 cups (500ml) beef stock, heated

Preheat the oven to 240°C.
Place the beef in a large flameproof roasting pan and rub all over with a little oil, then season with sea salt and pepper and scatter with thyme leaves. Roast in the oven on the middle shelf for 15 minutes. Reduce the oven temperature to 190°C and cook for a further 1 hour for medium-rare or until done to your liking.
Remove the pan from the oven and transfer the beef to a plate, cover loosely with foil and set aside in a warm place to rest for 30 minutes.
Meanwhile, for the gravy, drain and discard all but 1 tbs of fat from the pan. Place the pan over medium heat, add onion and cook for 5 minutes or until softened. Stir in flour and cook for 1 minute, then gradually stir in wine, scraping bits from the base of the pan. Bring to the boil and cook until reduced by half. Stir in the stock, return to the boil, then reduce the heat to low and simmer for 20 minutes or until thickened. Season.
Tip any resting juices from the beef into gravy and strain. Garnish beef with extra thyme. Cut meat away from bones. Carve the meat and serve with the gravy.
* Ask your butcher to 'chine' the rib of beef, which means to semi-detach the backbone from the ribs, making the joint easier to carve.

rack of pork with cider apples
Serves 6

2kg rack of pork
Olive oil, to rub
4 green apples (about 750g total), peeled, cored, cut into thick wedges
⅓ cup (75g) caster sugar
1 cinnamon quill
2 tsp chopped sage leaves
400ml good-quality alcoholic cider
100g unsalted butter, chopped
200ml good-quality chicken stock
Roasted parsnips and steamed broccoli, to serve

Preheat the oven to 220°C.
Place the pork in a roasting pan, skin-side up, then rub the skin with a little oil and sprinkle generously with sea salt. Roast for 15 minutes, then reduce oven temperature to 180°C and roast for 1¼-1½ hours or until juices run clear when a skewer is inserted into the centre.
Meanwhile, place the apple, sugar, cinnamon, sage and 200ml cider in a saucepan over low heat, cover and cook for 20-25 minutes until the apple is soft. Allow to cool slightly. Remove and discard the cinnamon quill, then process the mixture in a food processor with 50g of the butter until smooth (you may need to add more sugar depending on the tartness of the apples).
Transfer the cooked pork to a platter, cover loosely with foil and set aside to rest while you make the gravy.
Skim any excess fat from the pan juices and place the pan over medium heat. Add the stock and remaining cider and cook for 2-3 minutes, stirring and scraping any brown bits from the base of the pan. Whisk in the remaining 50g butter, then strain into a jug.
Carve the pork and serve with the pureed cider apples, gravy, roasted parsnips and steamed broccoli.

roasts.

Creamy pot-roast chicken

creamy pot-roast chicken
Serves 4-6

80g unsalted butter, softened
1 red chilli, seeds removed, chopped, plus extra ½ chilli, sliced
2 tbs finely chopped flat-leaf parsley leaves
4 large garlic cloves, 3 crushed, 1 thinly sliced
1 lemon
1.8kg whole chicken
2 tbs olive oil
8 large eschalots, thinly sliced
½ large butternut pumpkin (about 600g), peeled, cut into wedges
200ml white wine
2 cups (500ml) chicken stock, heated
100g creme fraiche
Tarragon leaves, to garnish (optional)

Preheat the oven to 200°C.
  Place 60g of the butter, chopped chilli, parsley, crushed garlic and grated zest of the lemon in a bowl and combine. Ease the skin away from the chicken breast with your fingers, starting from the neck end. Spoon butter mixture under the skin, smoothing skin with your fingers to cover breasts evenly.
  Season chicken inside and out. Halve the lemon, squeeze juice into cavity, then place halves inside. Tie legs with string.
  Heat remaining 20g butter and oil in a flameproof casserole over medium-high heat. Add eschalot and cook, stirring, for 5 minutes until softened. Add sliced chilli and garlic for the final 2 minutes.
  Add the pumpkin and stir. Nestle the chicken among the vegetables. Pour over the wine and cook for 2 minutes or until reduced by half. Add stock, bring to the boil, then cover with foil and roast in the oven for 1 hour.
  Uncover, then cook for a further 20-25 minutes or until chicken is cooked through and golden and the juices from the thigh run clear when pierced with a skewer. Transfer chicken and vegetables to a dish, loosely covered with foil, to rest.
  Place casserole over medium heat, skim any fat from surface, then simmer for 5 minutes to reduce the juices a little. Stir in creme fraiche, season, then spoon sauce over the chicken and scatter with tarragon leaves.

greek lamb with crispy potatoes
Serves 4

3 garlic cloves, crushed
2 tbs chopped rosemary leaves
1 lemon, sliced
¼ cup (60ml) olive oil
4 x 4-cutlet lamb racks
10 chat potatoes
150g vine-ripened cherry tomatoes
1 cup (160g) pitted kalamata olives
Good-quality mint sauce, to serve (optional)

Combine garlic with rosemary, lemon and 2 tablespoons of the oil, in a bowl. Add lamb, season with salt and pepper, and toss to coat. Marinate for 15 minutes.
  Meanwhile, preheat the oven to 180°C. Par-cook the potatoes in a pan of boiling salted water for 5-6 minutes, then drain.
  Flatten each potato with a potato masher and place in an oiled roasting pan. Drizzle with remaining 1 tablespoon of olive oil and season well. Roast in the oven for 15 minutes or until golden.
  Meanwhile, heat a large frypan over medium-high heat. Sear lamb on all sides, then place lamb and any pan juices on the potatoes with lemon slices. Roast for 10 minutes for medium-rare, or until done to your liking. Remove lamb, cover loosely with foil and rest for 5 minutes.
  Meanwhile, add the tomatoes and olives to the potatoes, then return the pan to the oven for a further 5 minutes until tomatoes soften. Serve with mint sauce, if desired.

Greek lamb with crispy potatoes

Roast duck with star anise & orange sauce

roasts.

roast duck with star anise & orange sauce
Serves 4

2kg whole duck*
Pared rind of 1 orange, cut into long thin strips, plus the juice of 2-3 oranges (150ml)
25g raw sugar
1/3 cup (80ml) red wine vinegar
2 cups (500ml) chicken stock
2 tsp redcurrant jelly*
2 star anise, broken into separate 'petals'
1/4 cup (60ml) lemon juice
1 tbs Cointreau
1 tsp arrowroot*
Green peas, potato mash and watercress, to serve

Wash duck and dry well with paper towel. Place on a paper towel-lined tray and stand in a cool, dry place for 1 hour. This will help make the skin even crispier.

Preheat oven to 230°C. Season cavity and sprinkle plenty of salt over skin. Place on a rack over a roasting pan. Roast for 20 minutes, then reduce oven to 180°C and roast for a further 40 minutes until golden and cooked through.

Meanwhile, drop orange rind into a pan of boiling water for 5 seconds, then drain and refresh in cold water. Leave to drain on paper towel.

Combine the sugar and vinegar in a small saucepan over low heat, stirring to dissolve sugar. Bring to boil and cook for 6 minutes or until mixture is an amber syrup. Add stock, jelly, orange juice and star anise. Bring to the boil and simmer rapidly for 25-30 minutes until reduced by three-quarters (to about 150ml). Stir in lemon juice and Cointreau and season.

Mix arrowroot with 1 tbs cold water. Stir into sauce, simmer for 1 minute until thickened, then add rind and keep warm.

Transfer duck to a board, cover loosely with foil and rest for 10 minutes. To carve, cut off legs and halve at joints. Cut breasts away from bone and slice thinly. Serve with sauce, peas, mash and watercress.
* Ducks are from selected butchers and poultry shops. Redcurrant jelly and arrowroot are from supermarkets.

Rosemary salt roast lamb with boulangère potatoes

rosemary salt roast lamb with boulangère potatoes
Serves 6

2kg leg of lamb
1 tbs chopped rosemary leaves, plus extra leaves to garnish (optional)
2 garlic cloves, roughly chopped
Olive oil, to drizzle
1 tsp plain flour
600ml lamb or chicken stock, heated

Boulangère potatoes
100ml duck fat
2 small onions, thinly sliced
2 tbs thyme leaves
100ml dry white wine
8 desiree potatoes, peeled, cut into 3-4mm slices (a mandoline is ideal)
About 300ml chicken stock, heated

Preheat oven to 200°C. Grease a 2L baking dish. Using a small, sharp knife, make small 2.5cm-deep slits all over the leg, 5cm apart. Place rosemary, 1 tbs sea salt, garlic and black pepper in a mortar and pestle and crush until it's a rough green salt. Rub rosemary salt all over lamb, pushing it into the slits. Set aside.

Place lamb in a roasting pan, drizzle with oil. Roast in the oven for 15 minutes.

Meanwhile, for boulangère potatoes, heat duck fat in a large frypan over medium-low heat. Add onion and thyme and cook, stirring, for 8 minutes until soft. Add wine and simmer for 2-3 minutes until almost evaporated. Add potato and stir to coat. Layer potato mixture in baking dish, overlapping in a circular pattern. Pour over enough stock to submerge potatoes. Cover surface closely with baking paper. Cover pan with foil.

Reduce oven to 180°C. Roast lamb for 1 1/4 hours, adding potatoes for final 30 minutes. Remove lamb from oven and transfer to a board, loosely covered with foil. Rest for 15-20 minutes. Remove foil and paper from potatoes and bake for a further 20 minutes until stock is absorbed and potato is golden.

Meanwhile, skim excess fat from pan and place over medium heat. Stir in flour using a wooden spoon. Gradually add stock, scraping any bits from the base of the pan. Gently simmer until thickened. Season and strain. Carve lamb and serve with gravy and potatoes. **d.**

Rigatoni with sausage & fennel ragu

pasta

- **77** spaghetti with spicy bolognese
- **77** rigatoni with sausage & fennel ragu
- **77** pumpkin, sage & ricotta lasagne
- **78** pasta with garlic prawns
- **78** perfect potato gnocchi
- **81** pumpkin & ricotta ravioli with chestnut butter sauce
- **81** spaghetti puttanesca
- **82** cauliflower pasta
- **82** creamy bacon, leek & pea farfalle
- **85** chargrilled vegetable, mozzarella & prosciutto pasta bake
- **85** cheesy pumpkin pasta bake

Pumpkin, sage & ricotta lasagne

Spaghetti with spicy bolognese

pasta.

spaghetti with spicy bolognese
Serves 4

2 tbs olive oil
1 small red onion, finely chopped
2 garlic cloves, finely chopped
4 slices hot pancetta*, finely chopped
500g beef mince
1 tsp dried oregano
2 tbs tomato paste
1 cup (250ml) red wine
1 cup (250ml) beef stock
1/4 cup (60ml) tomato sauce (ketchup)
1 tbs sweet chilli sauce
400g can chopped tomatoes
400g spaghetti
2 tbs finely chopped flat-leaf parsley leaves
Shaved parmesan and basil leaves, to serve

Heat the olive oil in a large saucepan over medium heat. Add the onion, garlic and pancetta and cook, stirring, for 2-3 minutes until the onion softens slightly. Add the beef and cook, stirring, for 3-4 minutes until browned all over. Add the dried oregano and tomato paste and cook for a further 1 minute, then add the red wine and bring to the boil. Add the beef stock, tomato sauce, sweet chilli sauce and chopped tomatoes, then season to taste with sea salt and freshly ground black pepper. Reduce the heat to low and simmer for 30 minutes until the bolognese thickens.

Meanwhile, cook the pasta in a large pan of boiling salted water according to the packet instructions, then drain.

Add the pasta and chopped parsley to the sauce and toss well to combine. Divide pasta among bowls, then served topped with parmesan and basil.

* From delis and selected butchers.

rigatoni with sausage & fennel ragu
Serves 4

500g rigatoni or other short pasta
2 tbs olive oil
1 onion, finely chopped
2 garlic cloves, finely chopped
2 tsp fennel seeds
400g good-quality spicy Italian sausages
400g can chopped tomatoes
2 tbs tomato paste
1 1/2 cups (375ml) beef or chicken stock, heated
2 tbs chopped flat-leaf parsley leaves
25g parmesan, grated

Heat the oil in a saucepan over low heat. Add the onion and cook for 5 minutes until it begins to soften. Stir in the garlic and fennel seeds, then cook for a further 1 minute.

Split open the sausages, add the meat to the onion and gently cook, breaking it up with a wooden spoon, until golden. Add the tomatoes, paste and stock and season well. Simmer for 15-20 minutes until the sauce has thickened.

Meanwhile, cook the pasta in a large pan of boiling salted water according to the packet instructions, then drain.

Toss the pasta with the sausage ragu and chopped parsley. Sprinkle with the parmesan to serve.

pumpkin, sage & ricotta lasagne
Serves 4

1.2kg butternut pumpkin, peeled, cut into 2cm pieces
2 tbs olive oil
1/2 tsp dried chilli flakes
1 tbs chopped sage leaves, plus 12 whole leaves to serve
1/4 tsp freshly grated nutmeg
350g fresh ricotta
1 egg
1 cup (80g) grated parmesan, plus extra to serve
8 fresh lasagne sheets
100g unsalted butter
2 tbs chopped walnuts

Preheat the oven to 190°C.

Place the pumpkin on a baking tray, drizzle with oil, sprinkle with chilli flakes and season with sea salt and freshly ground black pepper. Cover with foil and roast for 25 minutes or until the pumpkin is tender. Allow to cool slightly.

Puree pumpkin in a food processor with the chopped sage and nutmeg. Set aside. Clean processor, then process the ricotta, egg, 1/2 cup (40g) parmesan, salt and pepper.

Lightly grease a 24cm-square baking dish. Lay 2 lasagne sheets over the base and spread with half the pumpkin. Add another layer of lasagne sheets, then spread with half the ricotta. Repeat process, then sprinkle final layer of ricotta with remaining parmesan. Lay a sheet of baking paper over surface, cover dish with foil and bake for 35 minutes. Remove foil and paper and bake for a further 15 minutes or until golden. Stand for 5 minutes.

Meanwhile, heat the butter, sage and walnuts in a pan over medium heat for 1-2 minutes until the butter starts to foam. Remove from the heat.

Serve the lasagne drizzled with sage butter, scattered with extra parmesan.

pasta.

Pasta with garlic prawns

pasta with garlic prawns
Serves 4

500g casarecci* or
   other short pasta
1 tbs olive oil
3 garlic cloves, crushed
20 green prawns, peeled
   (tails intact), deveined
¼ tsp dried chilli flakes
2 tbs chopped parsley leaves
Juice and zest of
   1 large lemon
1 cup (250ml) white wine
100g chilled unsalted butter,
   cut into small pieces
1 tbs baby capers,
   rinsed

Cook the pasta in a large saucepan of boiling salted water following packet instructions.

Meanwhile, gently heat the olive oil and garlic in a frypan over low heat. When the oil is hot, add the prawns, chilli and half the parsley, increase the heat to high and cook for 2-3 minutes.

Add the lemon juice and white wine to the pan and increase the heat to medium. Cook for 2 minutes until the sauce is slightly reduced. Stir in the butter, lemon zest and capers until well combined. Drain the pasta and add to the pan. Toss together until well combined. Serve garnished with the remaining chopped parsley.

* Casarecci is from selected gourmet food stores and Italian grocers.

perfect potato gnocchi
Serves 6

1.5kg floury potatoes (such as sebago)
¼ tsp freshly grated nutmeg
2 eggs, beaten
2⅓ cups (350g) plain flour,
   plus extra to dust
3 cups (750ml) roasted-tomato sugo
   (see Basics, p 136) or good-quality
   tomato pasta sauce, heated
Grated parmesan and oregano leaves,
   to serve

Place the potatoes in a pan of cold water, bring to the boil, then cook for 15 minutes until tender. Drain, return to the pan over low heat and toss for 1 minute to remove any moisture.

Cool slightly, then peel and pass the potatoes through a potato ricer (from kitchenware shops) into a large bowl. Add the nutmeg, eggs and 1 tbs salt, then sift in the flour. Using your hands, gently mix until a soft dough forms, adding a little extra flour if it's too sticky – don't overwork or the gnocchi will be tough. Turn onto a floured bench and dust hands with flour.

Take a cupful of dough, form into a log, then use a rolling pin to gently roll into a 2cm-thick rectangle. Use a sharp knife to cut into 2cm-wide strips, then cut strips into 2cm lengths. Place gnocchi on a tray dusted with flour in a single layer, then repeat with remaining dough. At this stage, you can set gnocchi aside, covered with a tea towel, for 2-3 hours until ready to cook.

Cook gnocchi, in 2 batches, in a large pan of boiling salted water. As soon as they rise to the surface (30-60 seconds), transfer to a tray with a slotted spoon. Toss briefly in a deep frypan with the sugo or pasta sauce. Serve immediately with parmesan and oregano leaves.

Perfect potato gnocchi

Pumpkin & ricotta ravioli with chestnut butter sauce

pasta.

pumpkin & ricotta ravioli with chestnut butter sauce
Serves 4

½ butternut pumpkin (about 450g), peeled, cut into 2cm pieces
1 tbs olive oil
1 garlic clove, crushed
150g fresh ricotta, drained
½ tbs chopped sage leaves
75g grated parmesan, plus extra to serve
48 wonton wrappers*

Chestnut butter sauce
2 tbs extra virgin olive oil
100g unsalted butter
150g peeled, cooked fresh or vacuum-packed chestnuts*, chopped
2 tbs chopped sage leaves

Preheat oven to 190°C. Place pumpkin and oil in a roasting pan, season and toss. Roast for 20 minutes, add garlic and cook for a further 10 minutes until tender. Cool.

Pulse pumpkin in clean food processor until smooth. Place in a bowl, stir in ricotta, sage and parmesan. Season.

Lay 24 wonton wrappers on a clean surface. Place 1 tbs pumpkin mixture in the centre of each wrapper. Brush edges of wrappers with water, then place another wrapper on top, pressing to seal and pushing out any air. Trim with a 7cm fluted cutter. Repeat to make 24 ravioli.

Bring a large saucepan of salted water to the boil. Cook ravioli, in batches, for 3 minutes until pasta is cooked and filling is set. Remove with a slotted spoon and set aside.

Meanwhile, for the sauce, heat the oil and butter in a large frypan over medium-low heat. Add chestnuts and cook for 5 minutes until foamy and starting to colour. Stir in the sage leaves, season, then add pasta to the frypan and carefully toss. Serve with extra grated parmesan.
* Wonton wrappers are from selected supermarkets and Asian food shops. Fresh chestnuts are available in season from greengrocers. Cooked chestnuts are from gourmet shops and delis.

Spaghetti puttanesca

spaghetti puttanesca
Serves 4

¼ olive or plain ciabatta loaf
100ml olive oil
1 tbs chopped thyme leaves, plus thyme sprigs to serve
1 large tomato
2 red onions, thinly sliced
4 garlic cloves, finely chopped
Pinch of dried chilli flakes
12 anchovy fillets in oil, drained, chopped
200g semidried tomatoes, halved
200g pitted kalamata olives
400g spaghetti

Preheat oven to 180°C. Whiz ciabatta in a food processor until coarse crumbs. Spread onto a baking tray lined with foil, drizzle with ¼ cup (60ml) oil, scatter with thyme and season. Bake for 10 minutes until golden and crisp, then set aside.

Meanwhile, cut a small cross in base of tomato. Plunge into boiling water for 30 seconds, then refresh in iced water. Peel and halve. Scoop out seeds. Finely chop.

Place remaining 2 tbs oil in a large pan over medium heat. Cook onion, stirring, for 3-4 minutes until soft. Add chopped tomato, garlic, chilli and anchovies. Cook, stirring, for 3-4 minutes until anchovies dissolve and tomato has broken down. Add semidried tomatoes and olives and stir for 1-2 minutes to warm through.

Meanwhile, cook pasta in a large pan of boiling salted water according to packet instructions. Drain. Toss in sauce. Scatter with breadcrumbs and thyme sprigs.

pasta.

Cauliflower pasta

cauliflower pasta
Serves 4-6

500g penne
700g cauliflower, cut into small florets, small green leaves reserved
2 tbs olive oil
1 onion, finely chopped
2 garlic cloves, finely chopped
1 long red chilli, halved, seeds removed, finely chopped
2 anchovy fillets
2 tbs tomato paste
4 ripe tomatoes, roughly chopped
Grated parmesan, to serve

Cook the pasta in a large saucepan of boiling lightly salted water for 6 minutes. Add the cauliflower and cook for a further 5-6 minutes (add the cauliflower leaves in the last 2 minutes of cooking) or until tender and the pasta is al dente.

Meanwhile, heat the oil in a medium non-stick frypan. Reduce heat to medium-low, add the onion, garlic, chilli and anchovy and cook, stirring, for 5 minutes or until soft. Add the tomato paste and stir to combine. Add the tomatoes and cook for 3-5 minutes or until softened and pulpy. Season with salt and pepper.

Drain the pasta mixture, reserving some of the cooking water. Stir the cauliflower, leaves and pasta into the tomato mixture and loosen with a little of the reserved water. Divide between bowls and serve with parmesan.

creamy bacon, leek & pea farfalle
Serves 4

200g farfalle (bowtie) pasta
1 tbs olive oil, plus extra to toss
20g unsalted butter
2 garlic cloves, finely chopped
1 leek (white part only), sliced
8 pancetta slices (about 100g total), rind removed, chopped
1 cup (120g) frozen peas
300ml thickened cream
2 eggs
$^1/_3$ cup (25g) grated parmesan, plus extra to serve
$^1/_4$ cup finely shredded mint leaves

Cook the pasta in a large saucepan of boiling salted water according to packet instructions. Drain well, reserving 3-4 tablespoons of cooking water. Toss the pasta with a little oil.

Heat the oil and butter in a small saucepan over medium heat. Add the garlic, leek and pancetta and cook for 2-3 minutes until leek has softened and pancetta starts to crisp. Add the peas and cook for 1-2 minutes to defrost and heat through.

Place the cream, egg and parmesan in a jug, season with black pepper and stir well to combine.

Add pasta and cream mixture to the pan and stir to combine well. (The egg in the cream mixture will cook in the hot pasta.) Add a little of the cooking water to loosen the sauce if necessary. Stir in the shredded mint, then serve with lots of extra parmesan.

Creamy bacon, leek & pea farfalle

Chargrilled vegetable, mozzarella & protsciutto pasta bake

pasta.

Cheesy pumpkin pasta bake

chargrilled vegetable, mozzarella & prosciutto pasta bake
Serves 4

400g rigatoni or penne pasta
190g jar good-quality sundried tomato pesto
250g mascarpone cheese
2 x 280g jars chargrilled vegetables
300g buffalo mozzarella* or bocconcini, drained, sliced
8 slices prosciutto, torn
Basil leaves, to garnish

Preheat the grill to medium.
 Cook the pasta in a large saucepan of boiling salted water according to packet instructions. Drain well, then return the pasta to the pan.
 Add the pesto and mascarpone and stir until the pasta is coated in the sauce. Stir in the chargrilled vegetables. Transfer the pasta mixture to a medium ovenproof dish. Scatter with mozzarella and season well. Place under the grill for 5-6 minutes until the mozzarella is melted and golden.
 Dot the top with prosciutto and scatter with basil leaves.
* From delis and gourmet food shops.

cheesy pumpkin pasta bake
Serves 6

¼ cup (60ml) olive oil
1 onion, finely chopped
3 garlic cloves, finely chopped
100g bacon or pancetta, chopped
800g pumpkin, peeled, cut into 2cm cubes (to give 3 cups)
¼ tsp dried chilli flakes
3 cups (750ml) chicken stock
300g macaroni
300ml pure (thin) cream
1 tbs chopped rosemary
2 cups (140g) fresh breadcrumbs
2 tsp grated lemon zest
1 cup flat-leaf parsley leaves
1¼ cups (150g) grated cheddar

Preheat the oven to 200°C. Heat 1 tbs oil in a frypan over medium heat. Add the onion, garlic and bacon or pancetta and cook, stirring, for 2-3 minutes until the onion softens slightly. Add the pumpkin and dried chilli flakes, stir to combine, then add half the chicken stock and cook for 5-6 minutes until the pumpkin begins to soften.
 Stir in pasta, cream, rosemary and remaining chicken stock. Season to taste with sea salt and freshly ground black pepper, bring to a simmer, then reduce the heat to low and cook for about 8-10 minutes until the pasta and pumpkin are tender.
 Meanwhile, place the breadcrumbs, lemon zest, flat-leaf parsley and a third of the cheese in a food processor and process until you have fine crumbs. Add the remaining 2 tablespoons olive oil and pulse to combine.
 Stir the remaining cheese into the pasta mixture, then transfer to a baking dish. Scatter with the crumbs, then bake for 15 minutes or until golden. **d.**

Indian spiced eggplant

spice

89 chicken biryani
89 indian spiced eggplant
89 coconut lamb curry
90 chilli for a crowd
90 rogan josh-braised chicken
93 aromatic duck curry
93 easy fish tagine
94 chicken laksa
94 red-cooked beef with gai lan
97 thai pork larb
97 chicken & asparagus green curry

Coconut lamb curry

Chicken biryani

spice.

chicken biryani
Serves 4

1 tbs unsalted butter
1/4 cup (60ml) olive oil
8 chicken thigh cutlets (on the bone), with skin
1 large onion, thinly sliced
1 garlic clove, sliced
3 tbs medium curry paste
1 3/4 cups (350g) basmati rice
1/3 cup (25g) flaked almonds, toasted
3 cups (750ml) vegetable stock, heated
100g baby green beans, put through a beaner or chopped
1 cup (120g) frozen peas
Small bunch coriander, leaves chopped

Preheat the oven to 180°C. Heat the butter and 2 tbs of the oil in a flameproof casserole over medium-high heat. Cook chicken, in batches, for 2-3 minutes each side until browned. Remove from the pan and set aside.

Reduce the heat to medium-low, add the onion and garlic and cook, stirring, for 5 minutes until softened. Stir in the curry paste and cook, stirring, for 3 minutes until fragrant.

Add the remaining 1 tbs oil to casserole. Stir in the rice to coat in the oil and spicy onion and cook for 1 minute until coated. Stir in half the almonds and pour in the stock. Top with chicken and cover with foil and a lid. Cook in oven for 25 minutes, adding beans and peas in the final 10 minutes of cooking time, until the rice is tender and the chicken is cooked through. Stir in coriander, then serve scattered with remaining almonds.

indian spiced eggplant
Serves 6

2 eggplants, cut into 2cm cubes
1/4 cup (60ml) sunflower oil
4cm piece ginger, finely chopped
2 tsp ground coriander
1 1/2 tsp cumin seeds
1 tsp nigella seeds*
1/2 tsp fennel seeds
1/2 tsp mustard seeds
1/2 tsp fenugreek seeds
1/2 tsp hot chilli powder
1/2 tsp ground turmeric
400g can chopped tomatoes
Chopped coriander leaves, to garnish

Place the eggplant in a large colander and sprinkle liberally with salt. Set aside to drain for 10 minutes, then rinse well and pat dry well with paper towel.

Heat the oil in a wok over medium heat. Add the ginger and spices and cook, stirring, for 2-3 minutes until fragrant. Add the eggplant, in batches, and cook, stirring, for 5 minutes or until eggplant is slightly softened, then transfer to a plate. Return all eggplant to wok, then stir in the tomatoes and 1 cup (250ml) water. Bring to the boil, then reduce the heat to low and simmer for 12-15 minutes until the eggplant is tender and the sauce has thickened. Season with salt and serve garnished with chopped coriander.
* Nigella seeds are available from Indian and Asian food shops.

coconut lamb curry
Serves 6

2 tbs ghee*
800g diced lamb shoulder
1 onion, thinly sliced
3 garlic cloves, thinly sliced
1 tbs grated ginger
1 long red chilli, deseeded, chopped
1 tsp ground turmeric
10 fresh curry leaves*
400g can chopped tomatoes
2 cups (500ml) lamb or beef stock
1/2 cup (125ml) coconut cream
2 tbs chopped coriander leaves, plus extra sprigs, to serve
Rice, chutney and raitas, to serve

Curry powder
1/4 cup coriander seeds
1 tbs each cumin, fenugreek, mustard and cardamom seeds
8 cloves
5cm piece cinnamon quill
1 tsp dried chilli flakes (or to taste)
1/4 tsp ground nutmeg
1 tbs ground turmeric

For powder, dry-fry all seeds and cinnamon in a non-stick frypan over low heat for 1 minute until fragrant. Using a mortar and pestle, grind to a powder with chilli, nutmeg and turmeric. Set aside.

Heat 1 tbs ghee in a flameproof casserole over medium-high heat. Brown lamb, in batches, for 3-4 minutes. Remove with a slotted spoon. Set aside.

Add remaining 1 tbs ghee and onion to same pan, reduce heat to medium and stir for 2-3 minutes until softened. Add garlic, ginger, chilli, turmeric and curry leaves and cook for 1 minute until fragrant. Stir in 4 tbs curry powder. Add lamb, tomato and stock. Bring to a boil, then simmer, uncovered, over low heat for 1 1/2 hours until lamb is tender.

Stir in cream and coriander, then cook for a further 10 minutes or until the sauce has thickened. Serve with extra coriander, rice, chutney and raitas.
* Ghee is from supermarkets. Curry leaves are from greengrocers.

spice.

Rogan josh-braised chicken

rogan josh-braised chicken
Serves 6

100ml olive oil
2 large onions, finely sliced
2 celery stalks, finely chopped
4 garlic cloves, sliced
2.5cm piece ginger, grated
½ tsp ground turmeric
½ tsp chilli powder
1 tsp ground cumin
1 tsp pimenton (smoked paprika)*
1 tsp ground coriander
2 tsp garam masala
2 x 400g cans chopped tomatoes
300ml chicken stock, heated
1.8kg whole chicken, legs trussed
Steamed basmati rice, to serve

Preheat the oven to 160°C.

Heat ⅓ cup (80ml) of the olive oil in a heavy-based casserole (big enough to contain the chicken and with a tight-fitting lid) over medium heat. Add the onion and celery and cook, stirring, for 5 minutes until just starting to soften. Add the garlic and ginger and cook for a further 3 minutes.

Add the spices and cook for a further minute until fragrant, then add the tomatoes and stock. Season well, then place the chicken in the casserole. Season, cover with the lid and cook in the oven for 1 hour 30 minutes.

Remove the lid of the casserole and brush the skin of the chicken with the remaining 1 tbs of olive oil. Baste with the juices and return to the oven, uncovered, for a further hour or until the chicken's skin is golden.

Carefully remove the chicken from the casserole, tipping out any juices from inside the cavity, and place on a warmed serving plate, loosely covered in foil, to rest. Bring the sauce to a simmer and cook for 15-20 minutes until thickened. Serve the chicken with the rogan josh sauce and steamed rice.
* Available from gourmet food shops and selected delis.

chilli for a crowd
Serves 10

¼ cup (60ml) olive oil
2kg beef chuck steak, trimmed, cut into 2cm cubes
2 onions, chopped
150g piece pancetta, chopped
4 garlic cloves, finely chopped
2 tbs ground cumin
⅓ cup (4 tbs) tomato paste
1½ tsp chilli powder
2 tsp dried oregano
1 cup (250ml) red wine
700ml tomato passata* (sieved tomatoes)
2 tsp brown sugar
3 cups (750ml) beef stock
2 x 420g cans kidney beans, rinsed, drained
Flat-leaf parsley leaves, to garnish
Herbed rice and cornbread, to serve

Preheat the oven to 170°C.

Heat 2 tbs oil in a large flameproof casserole over high heat. Cook beef, in batches, until browned all over. Set aside.

Reduce heat to medium and add remaining 1 tbs oil to pan. Add onion, pancetta and garlic and cook, stirring, for 4-5 minutes until onion is starting to brown. Add cumin, tomato paste, chilli and oregano, and stir for 1 minute.

Add the wine, passata, sugar and stock, then season with salt and freshly ground black pepper. Return the beef to the pan and bring to the boil, then cover and cook in the oven for 3 hours until meat is tender and sauce has thickened.

Just before serving, stir in the beans and place over low heat to warm through. Garnish with parsley and serve with herbed rice and cornbread.
* Passata is available in bottles from supermarkets.

Chilli for a crowd

Aromatic duck curry

spice.

aromatic duck curry
Serves 4

250g chat potatoes
1 tbs sunflower oil
400ml can coconut milk
1 tbs light brown sugar, plus extra
1-2 tbs lime juice
1 tbs fish sauce
1 Chinese barbecued duck*, skin and bones discarded, meat chopped
Fried Asian shallots*, coriander leaves and steamed jasmine rice, to serve

Curry paste
1 tsp fennel seeds
1 tbs coriander seeds
2 tsp cumin seeds
2 tsp ground turmeric
3 pieces blade mace*
1/4 tsp white peppercorns
1 lemongrass stem
3 small red chillies, deseeded, chopped
65g eschalots, chopped
6 large garlic cloves, peeled
25g ginger, chopped
2 tbs sunflower oil

For paste, dry-fry seeds, turmeric and mace in a pan over medium heat, shaking for a few seconds until aromatic. Place in a mortar and pestle or spice grinder with peppercorns and grind to a powder.

Trim top third of lemongrass, peel and discard outer leaves and roughly chop tender core. Process in a food processor with chilli, eschalot, garlic, ginger, ground spices, 1/2 tsp salt and oil until a paste.

Place potatoes in a pan of salted water, bring to boil. Cook for 12-15 minutes until tender. Drain, cool. Thickly slice and cover.

Heat oil in a pan over medium heat, add curry paste and cook for 5 minutes. Add coconut milk and simmer for 10-12 minutes until thickened. Stir in sugar, lime juice and fish sauce, then taste and season with sugar and juice. Add duck and potato. Heat through for 3-4 minutes. Serve with shallots, coriander and rice.

* Chinese barbecued duck is from Asian barbecue shops. Fried Asian shallots are from Asian supermarkets. Mace is from spice shops.

Easy fish tagine

easy fish tagine
Serves 4

4 x 150g blue-eye fillets, skin off
500g King Edward potatoes, peeled, cut into 3cm pieces
2 tbs olive oil
4 garlic cloves, chopped
2 yellow capsicums, sliced
400g can chopped tomatoes
100ml vegetable stock
100g pitted green olives
Lemon wedges and coriander leaves, to serve

Marinade
2 tbs olive oil
1/2 tsp turmeric
1/2 tsp ground cinnamon
2 tsp ground cumin
1 tsp ground coriander
1/3 cup (80ml) lemon juice
2 large garlic cloves
1 cup roughly chopped coriander leaves

Place all marinade ingredients with 1 tsp salt in a mortar and pestle or mini food processor and grind until smooth. Rub half over fish. Cover and chill for 1 hour.

Meanwhile, place potato in a pan of salted water, bring to the boil and cook for 6-8 minutes until tender, then drain.

Place oil and garlic in a casserole over medium-low heat. Cook for 1-2 minutes, add capsicum and cook for 5 minutes. Add tomato and cook for 2 minutes. Stir in remaining marinade and stock. Season.

Place potatoes in a large frypan over medium-high heat. Top with half tomato mix, then fish. Add remaining tomato. Scatter with olives, cover and cook for 10-12 minutes until fish is just cooked through. Serve with lemon and coriander.

spice.

Chicken laksa

chicken laksa
Serves 4

1 tsp vegetable oil
2 eschalots, finely sliced
1 long red chilli, finely sliced
5cm piece ginger, sliced
1 tbs red curry paste
1 lemongrass stem (white part only), finely grated
2-3 chicken breasts (about 500g total), thinly sliced
2 cups (500ml) chicken stock
2 tbs fish sauce
1 tbs brown sugar
3 cups (90g) baby spinach leaves
270ml can coconut milk
Juice of 2 limes
150g thin rice noodles
Coriander leaves, to garnish
Lime wedges, to serve

Heat the oil in a saucepan over medium heat. Add the eschalot, chilli and ginger and cook, stirring, for 2 minutes.

Add the red curry paste, lemongrass, sliced chicken and chicken stock and bring to a simmer, skimming off any scum that rises to the top. Stir in the fish sauce and brown sugar and simmer, for 5 minutes or until the chicken is cooked through.

Add the baby spinach leaves, coconut milk and lime juice, stir to combine and warm through over medium-low heat until the spinach is wilted.

Meanwhile, prepare the rice noodles according to the packet instructions, then stir into the laksa.

To serve, ladle the laksa among 4 serving bowls, then garnish with coriander leaves. Serve with lime wedges to squeeze.

red-cooked beef with gai lan
Serves 4

This is a traditional slow-braised or 'red-cooked' dish, where beef is braised in a flavoured soy broth spiced with a whole host of Chinese seasonings and tea bags. Pork is also delicious cooked in this way. Freeze the leftover sauce and use it as the base for noodle soups.

1 tbs Sichuan peppercorns
6 star anise
4 large cinnamon quills
2 garlic cloves, sliced
4cm piece ginger, sliced
200ml light soy sauce
$1/3$ cup (80ml) dark soy sauce
3 dried long red chillies
150g yellow rock sugar* or brown sugar
2kg chuck steak, cut into 6-8cm pieces
2 lapsang souchong tea bags*
300g Chinese broccoli (gai lan), ends trimmed, steamed
Roasted kumara and carrots, to serve

Bring 1.5L of water to the boil in a medium-large saucepan over high heat. Add all the ingredients, except the tea bags and broccoli, then bring to a simmer. Reduce the heat to low, cover and cook, skimming any scum that rises to the top, for 2 hours. After $1^{1}/_{2}$ hours, add the tea bags.

Remove the tea bags from the broth and discard. Spoon the meat into bowls and pour over some of the sauce. Serve with steamed broccoli and roasted kumara and carrots.

* Yellow rock sugar is a dark yellow-coloured sugar, available from Asian food shops; substitute with brown sugar. Lapsang souchong is a smoky black tea, available from major supermarkets.

Red-cooked beef with gai lan

Chicken & asparagus green curry

spice.

Thai pork larb

thai pork larb
Serves 4

1 tbs peanut oil
1 red onion, sliced into thin wedges
1 tbs finely chopped lemongrass (white part only)
1 long red chilli, halved, finely chopped
1 tbs finely chopped ginger
2 garlic cloves, finely chopped
500g pork mince
2 tbs massaman curry paste
100g green beans, cut into 5cm lengths
1½ tbs fish sauce
2 tbs lime juice
1 tbs brown sugar
1 cup Thai basil leaves*
Cooked thin rice noodles, to serve

Heat the peanut oil in a wok over medium-high heat. Add the onion, lemongrass, chilli, ginger and garlic and cook for 1 minute or until fragrant. Add the pork and cook for 4-5 minutes or until cooked through.

Add the curry paste and cook, stirring, for 1-2 minutes or until fragrant. Add the beans, fish sauce, lime juice and sugar and cook, stirring, for 1-2 minutes or until the beans are just tender. Stir in half the basil leaves. Serve on rice noodles, topped with the remaining basil leaves.

* Thai basil is available from Asian food shops and greengrocers.

chicken & asparagus green curry
Serves 4

2 tbs sunflower oil
700g chicken breast fillets, cut into 2cm cubes
1 large onion, finely chopped
2 garlic cloves, crushed
1 lemongrass stem, outer leaves removed, quartered lengthways
4 tbs green curry paste
300ml coconut milk
1 cup (250ml) chicken stock
2 tbs bottled green peppercorns*, drained
2 kaffir lime leaves*
1 bunch asparagus, trimmed, halved
Fish sauce, to season
Coriander leaves, steamed jasmine rice and lime wedges, to serve

Heat the oil in a wok over high heat. Stir-fry the chicken, in batches, until golden all over, then transfer to a bowl and set aside.

Return the wok to high heat. Add the onion, garlic and lemongrass and stir-fry for 1 minute. Add curry paste and cook, stirring, for a further minute. Return the chicken to the wok and add the coconut milk, stock, peppercorns and kaffir lime leaves, then bring to the boil. Reduce the heat to medium and simmer for 2 minutes. Add the asparagus and cook for a further 2 minutes or until bright green. Season to taste with fish sauce.

Serve the curry, garnished with coriander leaves, with steamed jasmine rice and lime wedges.

* Green peppercorns are from supermarkets. Kaffir lime leaves are from Asian shops and greengrocers. **d.**

Spicy baked eggs

bakes

101 pasticcio (greek pasta bake)
101 spicy baked eggs
101 oven-baked risotto with prosciutto and fontina
102 lamb biryani
102 oven-baked sausages and balsamic tomatoes
105 sausage & porcini mushroom cannelloni
105 mexican polenta cobbler

Oven-baked risotto with prosciutto and fontina

Pasticcio (Greek pasta bake)

bakes.

pasticcio (greek pasta bake)
Serves 4

1 tbs olive oil, plus extra to brush
1 large onion, finely chopped
2 garlic cloves, crushed
500g lamb mince
1 tbs tomato paste
½ tsp ground cinnamon
400g can chopped tomatoes
½ cup (125ml) red wine
2 tsp dried oregano
250g thick Greek-style yoghurt
1 egg, beaten
100g mature cheddar, grated
100g feta, crumbled
350g macaroni
Green salad, to serve

Heat the oil in a large frypan over medium heat. Add the onion and garlic and cook, stirring, for 5 minutes until soft. Increase the heat to medium-high, add the lamb and cook, stirring, for 5 minutes until browned. Drain off the fat in a sieve, then return the meat to the pan.

Add the tomato paste and cinnamon and cook, stirring, for 1 minute. Stir in the tomatoes, wine and 200ml water. Add the oregano, season with salt and pepper and bring to the boil, then reduce the heat to medium-low and simmer, stirring occasionally, for 20 minutes until lamb is tender and sauce is thickened.

Preheat the oven to 180°C.

Process the yoghurt, egg and half the cheeses in a food processor until smooth. Season with pepper and set aside.

Cook the macaroni in a saucepan of boiling salted water following packet instructions. Drain well, then spoon half the pasta into a 6cm deep, 30cm x 20cm ovenproof dish. Season. Top with the mince and remaining macaroni. Press down, spoon over the yoghurt mixture and scatter with the remaining cheese. Bake for 25 minutes until golden and bubbling. Serve with a green salad.

spicy baked eggs
Serves 2

1½ tbs olive oil
2 eschalots, finely chopped
1 tsp sweet paprika
200g potatoes, peeled, cut into 1cm cubes
1½ cups (375ml) roasted tomato sugo (see Basics, p 136) or good-quality pasta sauce/passata
1 small red chilli, seeds removed, finely chopped
½ roasted capsicum*, chopped
60g baby spinach leaves
2 eggs
¼ cup (15g) fresh white breadcrumbs
1 tbs finely chopped flat-leaf parsley leaves

Preheat the oven to 180°C.

Heat 1 tbs oil in a large frypan over medium heat. Add the eschalot and cook for 1-2 minutes until softened. Add the sweet paprika and potato and stir to combine. Cook, stirring, for 10 minutes, adding a splash of water if they stick. Add the sugo, chilli and capsicum and bring to a simmer.

Stir through the spinach and heat until wilted. Divide mixture between two 350ml ovenproof dishes. Crack 1 egg into the centre of each dish and bake in the oven for 10-12 minutes until set.

Meanwhile, heat remaining ½ tbs olive oil in a frypan and cook the breadcrumbs until crisp. Add parsley and stir. When the baked eggs are ready, scatter with the breadcrumbs to serve.

* Available from delis and supermarkets.

oven-baked risotto with prosciutto and fontina
Serves 4

20g unsalted butter
2 tbs olive oil
1 large onion, finely chopped
1 garlic clove, crushed
2 cups (440g) arborio rice
1 tsp pimenton*
½ cup (125ml) dry sherry
1L (4 cups) chicken stock, heated
3 thyme sprigs, plus 1 tbs leaves
2 bunches asparagus, woody ends trimmed
100g thinly sliced prosciutto
½ cup (35g) grated fontina cheese*

Preheat the oven to 180°C.

Heat the butter and 1 tbs of the oil in a flameproof casserole over medium-low heat. Add the onion and garlic and cook, stirring, for 5 minutes until soft. Add the rice and pimenton and stir. Add the sherry, bring to the boil, then simmer, uncovered, for 1 minute until the sherry is absorbed. Add the stock and thyme sprigs. Cover and cook in the oven, stirring once, for 20-25 minutes or until the liquid is absorbed and the rice is tender.

Meanwhile, toss the asparagus in remaining 1 tbs oil and place on a baking tray with the prosciutto. Cook in the oven during the final 10 minutes of rice cooking time until the asparagus is cooked and the prosciutto is crisp. Chop the asparagus and break the prosciutto into shards. Just before serving, stir the fontina, asparagus and extra thyme leaves through the rice and top with the prosciutto.

* Pimenton (smoked paprika) and fontina (melting Italian cheese) are from delis.

bakes.

Lamb biryani

lamb biryani
Serves 6
Start this recipe a day ahead.

250g natural yoghurt, plus extra to serve
1 long green chilli, seeds removed, finely sliced
4 garlic cloves, crushed
50g piece ginger, grated
¼ tsp each ground cloves and ground cinnamon
2 tsp each ground cumin and ground coriander
750g lamb leg steaks, trimmed, cut into 3cm pieces
1¾ cups (350g) basmati rice
100ml milk
1 tsp saffron threads
4 tbs ghee*, plus extra 1 tbs
2 large onions, finely sliced
1 long cinnamon quill, broken into 3 pieces
12 cardamom pods, bruised
Chopped coriander leaves, to garnish
Indian pickles and naan bread, to serve

Combine the yoghurt, chilli, garlic, ginger, cloves, ground cinnamon, and half the cumin and half the ground coriander in a bowl. Season well, then add the lamb and toss to coat. Cover and chill at least 4 hours or overnight to marinate.

The next day, remove lamb from fridge and allow to return to room temperature. Rinse the rice, then soak in cold water for 30 minutes. Heat the milk until hot and stir in the saffron.

Meanwhile, preheat the oven to 150°C. Heat the ghee in a wide pan over medium heat. Add the onion and cook, stirring occasionally, for 15 minutes. Stir in remaining cumin and coriander and cook for 1 minute, then set aside.

Place the cinnamon, cardamom and a good pinch of salt in a saucepan, half-fill with water and bring to the boil. Add the rice, stir and return to the boil. Cook for 2 minutes. Drain and stir into the onion mixture.

Melt the extra 1 tbs ghee over low heat in a deep, 3L flameproof casserole with a tight-fitting lid. Spread a little of the rice in a thin layer on the bottom of the dish, then top with half the lamb and its marinade. Top with half the remaining rice, drizzle with half the saffron milk and place the remaining lamb and its marinade on top. Spread the last of the rice over and drizzle with the remaining saffron milk. Cover tightly with foil, then with the lid. Increase the heat to medium-high and cook for 30 seconds to build up steam. Transfer to the oven and bake for 30-35 minutes until the lamb and rice are tender.

Garnish with coriander. Serve with extra yoghurt, Indian pickles and naan.
* Ghee is clarified butter, from supermarkets.

oven-baked sausages and balsamic tomatoes
Serves 4

12 beef chipolatas (or 8 regular thin beef sausages)
6 garlic cloves, thinly sliced
2 red onions, cut into thin wedges
1 tbs olive oil
2 x 250g punnets cherry tomatoes, halved
¼ cup (60ml) balsamic vinegar
Basil leaves (torn if large), to serve

Preheat the oven to 180°C. Toss the sausages, garlic and onion with the oil in a large baking dish. Season, then bake, uncovered, for 15 minutes until the sausages are golden.

Add the tomatoes and balsamic vinegar and toss together gently. Return to the oven for a further 15 minutes or until tomatoes have started to break down and the sausages are cooked through. Stir in basil leaves to serve.

Oven-baked sausages and balsamic tomatoes

Sausage & porcini mushroom cannelloni

bakes.

sausage & porcini mushroom cannelloni
Serves 4

10g dried porcini mushrooms*
1/3 cup (80ml) extra virgin olive oil
1 onion, finely chopped
2 garlic cloves, crushed
500g pork sausages, meat removed from casing, broken into small pieces
1 tbs fresh thyme leaves or 1 tsp dried thyme leaves
2 tbs tomato paste
100ml chicken stock
6 fresh lasagne sheets
2 cups (500ml) roasted tomato sugo (see Basics, p 136) or good-quality pasta sauce/passata
1/2 cup (40g) grated parmesan
Basil leaves, to garnish

Preheat oven to 200°C. Grease a 20cm x 30cm ovenproof dish. Soak porcini in 150ml boiling water for 10 minutes.

Meanwhile, heat oil in a large frypan over medium heat. Add onion and garlic and cook for 10 minutes until soft and lightly browned. Add sausage meat and cook, breaking up with a wooden spoon, for 8-10 minutes until browned. Drain the mushrooms, reserving the liquid, and chop finely. Add to pan with thyme and cook for 2 minutes. Stir in tomato paste, reserved liquid and stock and simmer for 6-8 minutes until sauce is thickened and there is no liquid left. Set aside to cool.

Bring a large pan of salted water to the boil. Add the lasagne sheets, remove from the heat and leave for 5 minutes to soak. Drain, refresh under cold water, then separate the sheets and cut in half.

Spoon a thin layer of sugo over the base of the prepared dish. Spoon filling along 1 short edge of each lasagne sheet and roll up. Place, seam-side down, on sauce. Spoon over the remaining sugo. Scatter with the parmesan. Bake for 30 minutes until golden and bubbling. Garnish with basil leaves.

* Porcini mushrooms are from gourmet food shops and greengrocers.

Mexican polenta cobbler

mexican polenta cobbler
Serves 8

2 tbs sunflower oil
2 onions, finely chopped
4 garlic cloves, crushed
1 tsp dried chilli flakes
2 tsp ground cumin
1/2 tsp cayenne pepper
1kg lean beef mince
1 tbs tomato paste
2 tsp brown sugar
1 tsp dried oregano
300ml beef stock
400g can chopped tomatoes
2 roasted red capsicums*, finely chopped
2 x 400g cans kidney beans, rinsed, drained

Topping
1 1/3 cups (200g) plain flour
1 tsp baking powder
1 tbs brown sugar
1/4 tsp dried chilli flakes
1/2 cup (85g) polenta
70g cheddar, finely grated
1 egg
3/4 cup (185ml) milk
2 tbs sunflower oil
20g unsalted butter, melted

Heat oil in a pan over medium heat. Add onion and garlic and cook, stirring, for 10 minutes until lightly browned. Add chilli, cumin and cayenne and cook for 2-3 minutes. Increase heat to high, add beef and cook, breaking it up with a wooden spoon, for 5 minutes until browned. Add tomato paste, sugar, oregano, stock and tomato, bring to the boil, then simmer for 25 minutes until reduced and thick.

Stir in capsicum and beans. Season. Spoon into a 3L ovenproof dish.

Preheat oven to 220°C. For topping, sift flour, baking powder, sugar and a pinch of salt into a large bowl. Stir in chilli, polenta and 50g cheese. Beat egg, milk, oil and butter in a bowl, then stir into the dry ingredients. Drop 8 heaped tbs of mix around edge of dish, about 2.5cm apart. Sprinkle with remaining cheese. Bake for 20 minutes until topping is golden.

* From delis and supermarkets. **d.**

Baby vegetables

sides

109 twice-roasted potatoes with onion, herbs and chilli
109 baby vegetables
109 pan-fried brussels sprouts with bacon and almonds
110 whole baked pumpkin
110 field mushrooms stuffed with taleggio and prosciutto
113 'wild weed' salad with parmesan crisps
113 tartiflette (cheese & potato bake)
114 creamy celeriac & potato gratin
114 caponata

Pan-fried Brussels sprouts with bacon and almonds

Twice-roasted potatoes with onion, herbs and chilli

sides.

twice-roasted potatoes with onion, herbs and chilli
Serves 6
These golden potatoes are first baked whole, then torn into chunks so they become wonderfully crisp all over yet stay fluffy inside.

4-6 large King Edward or other floury potatoes, scrubbed
2 onions, thinly sliced
1 tbs finely chopped rosemary leaves
1 tbs thyme leaves
¼ tsp dried chilli flakes
3 garlic cloves, finely chopped
½ cup (125ml) extra virgin olive oil
40g unsalted butter, chopped

Preheat the oven to 200°C.
Prick the whole potatoes all over with a fork. Place on a baking tray, then roast in the oven for 1 hour until cooked.
Remove the tray from the oven (leaving the oven on) and allow to cool slightly. Once cool enough to handle, tear the potatoes into 3cm chunks.
Return the potato chunks to the baking tray and scatter with the onion, rosemary, thyme, chilli flakes and garlic. Drizzle with the oil and toss well to combine. Dot with pieces of butter and season with plenty of sea salt and freshly ground black pepper.
Roast the potatoes on the top shelf of the oven, turning regularly, for 15-20 minutes until crisp and golden.

baby vegetables
Serves 6

12 small kipfler potatoes, peeled
1 bunch baby (Dutch) carrots, scrubbed
3 baby fennel, trimmed, quartered
500g cauliflower, cut into florets
6 baby leeks (or 2 regular leeks, quartered)
150g snow peas
2 bunches baby beetroot (or 1 bunch regular beetroot, quartered)
Unsalted butter, to serve

Place the potatoes in a large saucepan of cold salted water and bring to the boil. Reduce the heat to medium and simmer for 5 minutes. Add the carrots, fennel and cauliflower, return to a simmer and cook for 3 minutes. Add the leek and cook for 3 minutes, then add the snow peas and cook for 1 minute or until all the vegetables are tender.
Meanwhile, cook the beetroot separately in a saucepan of boiling salted water for 10-12 minutes until tender. Cool slightly and peel. To serve, place hot vegetables on a platter and dot with pieces of butter.

pan-fried brussels sprouts with bacon and almonds
Serves 6

500g small Brussels sprouts, halved, outer leaves discarded
1 tbs olive oil
20g unsalted butter
8 bacon or pancetta slices, chopped
1 garlic clove, finely chopped
1 cup (160g) toasted almonds
2 tbs chopped flat-leaf parsley leaves

Blanch the Brussels sprouts in boiling salted water for 3-4 minutes until fork-tender. Drain and refresh under cold water.
Meanwhile, heat the oil and butter in a frypan over medium-high heat. Add the bacon and cook, stirring, for 2-3 minutes until it begins to crisp. Add the garlic and almonds and cook, stirring, for a further minute. Add the Brussels sprouts and toss for 2-3 minutes to warm through. Remove the pan from the heat, stir in the parsley, then serve.

sides.

Whole baked pumpkin

whole baked pumpkin
Serves 8

3kg jap pumpkin
30g unsalted butter
1 large onion, chopped
6 bacon rashers, finely chopped
3 cups (210g) fresh white breadcrumbs
2 garlic cloves, crushed
2 tbs chopped sage leaves
2 cups (240g) grated Swiss cheese
Olive oil, to brush
300ml pure (thin) cream

Preheat the oven to 180°C. Use a sharp knife to remove the top of the pumpkin and set aside. Scrape out and discard the seeds and fibre.

Melt the butter in a frypan over medium-low heat. Cook onion and bacon, stirring, for 5 minutes until onion softens. Add breadcrumbs and garlic and cook, stirring, until crumbs are well coated. Add the sage and season well. Set aside to cool slightly. Stir in cheese, then pack the stuffing into the pumpkin.

Lay a large lightly oiled sheet of foil over the base and sides of a baking tray and brush with a little olive oil. Place the pumpkin on the tray and pour enough cream into the cavity to fill to the top, pouring slowly to allow cream to be fully absorbed. Place the pumpkin lid on top and bring the sides of the foil up around the pumpkin.

Cover the top with more lightly oiled foil so the pumpkin is completely enclosed. Bake in the oven for 2 hours or until the pumpkin is tender (test by piercing the flesh with a skewer).

Serve the pumpkin and filling as an accompaniment to a roast dinner.

field mushrooms stuffed with taleggio and prosciutto
Serves 6

2 tbs olive oil, plus extra
 to drizzle
2 red onions, thinly sliced
6 field mushrooms, stalks trimmed
1/3 cup (50g) roughly chopped
 sundried tomatoes
8 prosciutto slices, cut into strips
250g Taleggio cheese*, sliced
1 tbs chopped flat-leaf parsley leaves

Heat the oil in a saucepan over medium heat. Add the onion and cook, stirring occasionally, for 10 minutes or until onion has caramelised.

Preheat the oven to 180°C. Place the mushrooms, stalk-side up, in a baking dish. Divide the tomato, onion and prosciutto among mushrooms, then top with cheese. Season, drizzle with extra oil, then bake for 20 minutes or until the mushrooms are tender and the cheese has melted. Garnish with parsley to serve.

* Taleggio is an Italian washed-rind cheese from delis; substitute other washed-rind cheese or brie.

Field mushrooms stuffed with Taleggio and prosciutto

'Wild weed' salad with parmesan crisps

sides.

Tartiflette (cheese & potato bake)

'wild weed' salad with parmesan crisps
Serves 6

1 cup (80g) freshly grated parmesan
1 tbs plain flour
²/₃ cup (160ml) olive oil
¼ cup (60ml) balsamic vinegar
8 cups (240g) mixed bitter salad leaves (such as radicchio, witlof and rocket) or mixed baby salad leaves (mesclun)

Preheat the oven to 180°C. Line 2 baking trays with baking paper.

Combine the grated parmesan and plain flour in a bowl. Spread six 6cm circles of the parmesan mixture onto the prepared trays, leaving room to spread. Bake in the oven for 3-5 minutes until golden. Remove from the oven and set aside to cool slightly, then break into shards. Set aside until ready to serve.

Whisk the olive oil and balsamic vinegar together in a small bowl. Season the dressing with salt and freshly ground black pepper, then toss with the mixed salad leaves and parmesan crisps in a bowl.

tartiflette (cheese & potato bake)
Serves 4-6

1kg pontiac potatoes, peeled, roughly chopped
50g unsalted butter
1 onion, chopped
2 garlic cloves, finely chopped
2 tsp chopped thyme leaves
200g piece speck*, cut into 1cm cubes
½ cup (125ml) dry white wine
200ml thickened cream
250g reblochon* or raclette* cheese, grated

Preheat the oven to 200°C.

Place the potato in a large pan of salted water, bring to the boil over high heat, then simmer for 3 minutes to par-cook. Drain well.

Melt the butter in a large frypan over medium-low heat. Add onion and cook, stirring, for 5 minutes or until soft. Add the garlic, thyme and speck then cook, stirring occasionally, for 5 minutes. Stir in the wine, cream, potato and most of the cheese.

Transfer the mixture to a large baking dish and top with the remaining cheese. Cover with baking paper to keep the cheese from sticking, then a layer of foil. Bake for 20 minutes, then remove foil and baking paper. Bake for a further 20 minutes or until bubbling and golden.
* Speck (a German-style smoked bacon) and raclette and reblochon cheeses are from delis and gourmet food shops. Substitute pancetta and gruyere.

sides.

Creamy celeriac & potato gratin

creamy celeriac & potato gratin
Serves 6

200ml vegetable stock
2 garlic cloves, lightly crushed
200ml thickened cream
1 tbs olive oil
1 onion, finely chopped
1 large celeriac bulb (about 650g), peeled, quartered, sliced 3mm thick (a mandoline is ideal)
650g potatoes, peeled, sliced 3mm thick (a mandoline is ideal)
1 tbs plain flour
1 tbs chopped flat-leaf parsley

Preheat the oven to 200°C. Grease a 1.2L ovenproof dish with butter.

Place the stock and garlic in a saucepan over medium-high heat and bring to the boil. Remove from the heat and stir in cream. Leave to cool.

Heat the oil in a frypan over low heat. Add the onion and cook, stirring, for 10 minutes or until very soft.

Place the celeriac and potato in a bowl and toss with the flour and parsley. Season with salt and pepper.

Place the celeriac and potato in the prepared dish and top with the onion. Strain the cream mixture, discarding the garlic, and pour over the gratin. Bake for 1¼ hours or until golden brown and bubbling and potato is cooked through.

caponata
Serves 6

This will keep for up to 5 days – store in an airtight container in the fridge. Add the fresh herbs just before serving.

½ cup (125ml) olive oil
2 red onions, chopped
2 celery stalks or 1 fennel bulb, chopped
1 red capsicum, seeds removed, cut into 1.5cm pieces
2 eggplants, cut into 1.5cm cubes
400g can chopped tomatoes, drained
100g large green olives
2 tbs capers
2 tbs caster sugar or to taste
100ml red or white wine vinegar
⅓ cup (50g) pine nuts
Basil or mint leaves (optional), to serve

Heat the olive oil in a large, deep frypan over medium heat. Add the onion, celery or fennel, capsicum, eggplant and ½ tsp salt and cook, stirring occasionally, for 20-25 minutes or until the capsicum and eggplant are very tender. Don't allow the mixture to catch on the bottom of the pan.

Stir in the tomatoes and continue to cook for a further 3 minutes. Add the olives, capers, sugar and vinegar to the pan and cook for 10 minutes or until most of the liquid has evaporated. Stir in the pine nuts. Add the basil or mint, stirring, until wilted, then remove from the heat. **d.**

Caponata

Chocolate banoffee pies

sweet pies & tarts

119 old-fashioned cherry pie
119 chocolate banoffee pies
119 red & white pear tart
120 treacle pecan tarts
120 walnut tart with prunes in armagnac
123 limoncello meringue pies
123 deep-dish apple, sour cream & nutmeg pie
124 cardamom custard tarts
124 apple & ginger strudel

Red & white pear tart

Old-fashioned cherry pie

sweet pies & tarts.

old-fashioned cherry pie
Serves 8-10

1kg frozen cherries, thawed
Lemon juice, to taste
3 tbs cornflour
100g caster sugar, plus extra to dust
½ vanilla bean, split, seeds scraped
1 tbs kirsch or cherry brandy (optional)

Pastry
2⅓ cups (350g) plain flour
150g chilled unsalted butter, chopped
100g caster sugar
50g almond meal
2 egg yolks
⅓ cup (80ml) chilled milk, plus extra to brush

For pastry, place flour and butter in a food processor and process until fine crumbs. Add sugar, meal, egg yolks and milk and process until mixture forms a smooth ball. Enclose in plastic wrap and chill for 30 minutes.

Meanwhile, toss cherries with a squeeze of lemon juice. Mix cornflour and 2 tbs water in a bowl to form a paste.

Place sugar and vanilla seeds in a pan over low heat until sugar dissolves. Increase the heat to medium and cook, without stirring, until a caramel forms. Add cherries, and liqueur if using. Cook, stirring, for 8 minutes until mixture is a loose, dark compote. Add cornflour paste and stir until thick enough to coat the back of the spoon. Set aside for 30 minutes to cool.

Preheat oven to 200°C. Place a baking sheet in oven. Roll out two-thirds of the pastry on a lightly floured surface to 3mm thick and use to line base and sides of a 23cm pie dish. Spread with filling.

Roll out remaining pastry to a 3mm-thick round. Brush edge of pastry case with water. Lay pastry top over the pie and crimp the edges to seal. Brush top with cold milk.

Put the pie dish on a hot baking sheet and bake for 30-35 minutes or until bubbling and golden. Rest for 10 minutes. Dust with extra caster sugar to serve.

chocolate banoffee pies
Makes 6

250g dark chocolate digestive biscuits
180g unsalted butter, chopped
1 tbs Dutch cocoa powder, plus extra to dust
½ firmly packed cup (110g) brown sugar
395g can condensed milk
75g good-quality dark chocolate, chopped
1 tbs golden syrup
300ml thickened cream
2 small bananas, sliced

Place the biscuits in a food processor and process until fine crumbs. Melt 80g of the butter and add to the biscuit crumbs with the cocoa. Process to combine. Press into six 10cm loose-bottomed tart pans. Chill for 20 minutes until bases are firm.

Place the sugar and remaining 100g of butter in a saucepan over low heat, stirring, until butter has melted. Add condensed milk and stir over low heat for 5 minutes or until the mixture is a thick, golden caramel. Remove from the heat, then add the chocolate and golden syrup, stirring to melt and combine. Fill tart shells with caramel mixture, smoothing tops with a palette knife. Chill for at least 1 hour to set.

Whip the cream until soft peaks form. When ready to serve, place the tarts on plates, top with sliced banana and whipped cream, then dust with cocoa.

red & white pear tart
Serves 6
You can poach the pears a day ahead, then chill until you're ready to bake.

4 small beurre bosc pears
½ lemon
2 cups (500ml) each white and red wine
2 cinnamon quills
1¼ cups (275g) caster sugar
1 vanilla bean, split, seeds scraped
45g unsalted butter, softened
½ cup (60g) almond meal
1 tsp vanilla extract
3 egg yolks
375g block frozen puff pastry, thawed
Icing sugar, to dust
Creme anglaise (see Basics, p 136) or ready-made vanilla custard, to serve

Peel pears, then rub with cut side of lemon to prevent browning. Halve and core, then rub with more lemon and set aside. Pare lemon rind, discarding fruit.

Place wines in 2 separate pans, each with 1 cinnamon quill, ½ cup (110g) caster sugar, half the rind and half the vanilla pod and seeds. Stir over low heat for 5 minutes to dissolve sugar, then add 4 pear halves to each pan. Poach over medium-low heat for 10 minutes or until just tender (this will depend on ripeness of the pears), then leave to cool in liquid.

Preheat oven to 180°C. Whiz butter, remaining ¼ cup (55g) sugar, meal, vanilla and egg yolks in a processor until combined. Set frangipane aside.

Roll out pastry on a lightly floured surface to a 12cm x 48cm rectangle. Place on a large lined baking tray. Prick area inside border with a fork and spread with frangipane. Pat pears dry with paper towel, reserving poaching liquid. Lay cut-side down on frangipane, alternating white and red pears head to tail about 1cm apart. Cut a strip of baking paper to fit over pears (leaving pastry border exposed) so pears don't dry out. Bake tart for 20-25 minutes until pastry is golden.

Brush pears with a little poaching liquid and dust with icing sugar. Cut into slices between each pear. Serve with custard.

sweet pies & tarts.

Treacle pecan tarts

treacle pecan tarts
Makes 8

220g golden syrup
40g unsalted butter, cubed
Juice and zest of 1/2 lemon
1/3 cup (25g) fresh white breadcrumbs
100g shelled pecans
Thickened cream or custard, to serve

Pastry
2 cups (300g) plain flour
1 tbs icing sugar
125g chilled unsalted butter, cubed
1 egg yolk

For pastry, process flour, sugar, butter and a pinch of salt in a food processor until fine crumbs. Add yolk and 2-3 tbs iced water and process until mixture comes together in a smooth ball. Enclose in plastic wrap and chill for 30 minutes.

Meanwhile, place golden syrup, butter, juice and zest in a small pan over medium heat and cook, stirring, until butter is melted and warmed through. Stir in breadcrumbs and pecans.

Preheat oven to 190°C. Lightly grease eight 8cm loose-bottomed tart pans. Roll out pastry on a lightly floured surface to 3mm thick and use to line pans. Trim edges. Chill for 10 minutes.

Preheat oven to 180°C. Line tarts with baking paper and fill with pastry weights or uncooked rice. Bake in the oven for 10 minutes. Remove paper and weights and return to oven for 5 minutes until dry and crisp. Spread filling in cases. Bake for 20 minutes until bubbling and golden brown. Cool before serving with cream.

walnut tart with prunes in armagnac
Serves 6
Soak the prunes a day ahead.

1 3/4 cups (175g) walnuts
2 eggs, plus 1 yolk mixed with milk
2 cups (440g) caster sugar
1 tsp vanilla extract
1 vanilla bean, split, seeds scraped
12 pitted prunes, soaked overnight in 1/4 cup (60ml) armagnac or brandy
Creme fraiche, to serve

Pastry
1 2/3 cups (250g) plain flour
2 tbs icing sugar, plus extra to dust
175g chilled unsalted butter, chopped
1 egg, plus 1 extra yolk

For pastry, place flour, sugar, butter and a pinch of salt in a food processor and process until fine crumbs. Add egg and yolk and pulse until mixture comes together in a smooth ball. Enclose in plastic wrap and chill for 30 minutes.

Preheat oven to 180°C. Grease a 36cm x 11cm rectangular loose-bottomed tart pan. Pulse nuts in a processor to coarse crumbs. Add eggs, 1 cup (220g) sugar and vanilla extract. Pulse to just combine.

Roll out two-thirds of dough to 5mm-thick and use to line the tart pan. Spread with the walnut mixture. Roll out the remaining dough to a 5mm-thick rectangle. Brush the edges of the case with water, then cover with the pastry top. Press edges together to seal and trim excess. Brush the top with egg yolk mixture, then bake for 30-35 minutes until golden.

Meanwhile, stir remaining 1 cup (220g) sugar, vanilla pod and seeds and 1 cup (250ml) water in a pan over low heat until sugar dissolves. Increase heat to medium and simmer for 5-6 minutes until reduced. Add prunes and soaking liquid, then cook over low heat for 3-4 minutes until syrupy. Set aside.

Cool tart in pan on a wire rack for 10 minutes, then remove from pan and dust with icing sugar. Serve warm with prunes and a dollop of creme fraiche.

Walnut tart with prunes in armagnac

Limoncello meringue pies

sweet pies & tarts.

limoncello meringue pies
Serves 8

¼ cup (35g) cornflour
⅓ cup (80ml) lemon juice
1 cup (220g) caster sugar
3 egg yolks, plus 2 eggwhites
¼ cup (60ml) limoncello liqueur
65g chilled unsalted butter, cubed

Pastry
2 cups (300g) plain flour
1 tbs icing sugar
125g chilled unsalted butter, cubed
1 egg yolk

For the pastry, process flour, icing sugar, butter and a pinch of salt in a food processor until the mixture resembles fine breadcrumbs. Add yolk and 2-3 tbs iced water and process until mixture comes together in a smooth ball. Enclose in plastic wrap and chill for 30 minutes.

Meanwhile, place cornflour in a bowl with 1 cup (250ml) water and stir until smooth. Place in a pan with lemon juice and ½ cup (110g) caster sugar and stir over low heat for 7-8 minutes until thickened. Remove from heat and add egg yolks, one at a time, combining well with a wooden spoon. Stir in limoncello and butter, then cover surface with a piece of baking paper (to prevent a skin from forming) and cool.

Lightly grease eight 8cm loose-bottomed tart pans. Roll out pastry on a lightly floured surface to 3mm thick and use to line tart pans. Trim edges and chill for 10 minutes.

Preheat oven to 180°C. Line tarts with baking paper and fill with pastry weights or uncooked rice. Bake in the oven for 10 minutes. Remove paper and weights and return to oven for 5 minutes until dry and crisp. Spread filling into pastry cases. Chill for 1 hour.

Preheat the oven to 200°C. Using electric beaters, beat eggwhites until soft peaks form. Gradually add the remaining sugar and beat until glossy and firm. Pipe or spoon onto tarts and bake for 5-6 minutes until top is golden. Cool slightly before serving.

Deep-dish apple, sour cream & nutmeg pie

deep-dish apple, sour cream & nutmeg pie
Serves 8-10

4 Granny Smith apples (about 750g total)
2 eggs
100g caster sugar, plus extra to sprinkle
1 tbs plain flour
300g sour cream
¼ small whole nutmeg, finely grated
Creme fraiche, to serve

Pastry
1¾ cups (260g) plain flour
½ cup (75g) self-raising flour
185g chilled unsalted butter, cubed
⅓ cup (75g) caster sugar
1 egg, beaten with 2 tbs water
1 tbs milk

For the pastry, sift the flours and a pinch of salt into a food processor. Add the butter and pulse until crumbs. Transfer to a bowl and stir in the sugar. Add the egg mixture and mix with a round-bladed knife until mixture comes together. Shape into a smooth ball. Divide into two pieces, one slightly larger than the other. Enclose in plastic wrap and chill for 30 minutes.

Roll out the larger pastry ball on a lightly floured surface to 3mm thick and use to line a lightly greased 23cm-wide, 4cm-deep loose-bottomed tart pan. Trim the edges. Chill for 20-30 minutes.

Preheat the oven to 180°C. Line the pastry case with baking paper and fill with pastry weights or uncooked rice. Bake for 10 minutes. Remove the paper and weights and return to oven for 10 minutes until lightly golden. Cool slightly. Loosen from the pan to make it easier to remove later.

Peel, core and cut the apples into 2cm-thick slices. Whisk the eggs, sugar and flour in a bowl. Whisk in the cream and nutmeg. Place a layer of apple over base of pastry case, then cover with a little cream mixture. Repeat until case is filled.

Roll out remaining pastry to a 3mm-thick disc. Brush edge of pastry case with water, cover with pastry disc and press edges to seal. Cut a slit in top. Bake for 1 hour. Set aside for ½ hour to cool. Remove from pan, sprinkle with sugar and serve warm with creme fraiche.

sweet pies & tarts.

Cardamom custard tarts

cardamom custard tarts
Makes 4

375g block frozen puff pastry, thawed
½ cup (110g) caster sugar
8 cardamom pods, lightly crushed
½ vanilla bean, split, seeds scraped
2 cups (500ml) milk
2 tbs cornflour
2 egg yolks
Icing sugar, to dust

Preheat the oven to 200°C. Lightly grease four 10cm quiche pans.
 Roll out the pastry on a lightly floured surface to 2mm-thick and use to line the tart pans. Chill for 15 minutes.
 Place the sugar, ½ cup (125ml) water, cardamom pods and vanilla pod and seeds in a saucepan over medium-high heat and bring to the boil, then reduce the heat to medium and simmer for 8 minutes or until the liquid becomes syrupy. Remove from the heat and pour half the syrup into a bowl (it will be used later to drizzle over the baked tarts). Discard the vanilla pod.
 Stir together the milk, cornflour and egg yolks in a bowl until the cornflour has dissolved. Add to the saucepan with the remaining cardamom syrup, increase the heat to medium and stir constantly for 4 minutes until the mixture thickens, making sure it doesn't burn. Remove from the heat and set aside to cool.
 Spread filling in pastry cases and bake for 20 minutes or until pastry is puffed and golden and custard dry to the touch. Serve dusted with icing sugar and drizzled with remaining cardamom syrup.

apple & ginger strudel
Serves 6-8

5 green apples (about 1kg total)
150g caster sugar
Grated zest and juice of 1 lemon
2 tbs chopped stem ginger in syrup*
2 tbs ginger marmalade*
 (or orange marmalade)
2 tbs sultanas
100g good-quality ginger biscuits*,
 finely crushed in a processor
10 sheets filo pastry
80g unsalted butter, melted, cooled
Icing sugar, to dust
Creme anglaise (see Basics, p 136),
 to serve

Preheat oven to 180°C. Peel, core and very thinly slice apples. Place in a large pan with sugar, lemon zest and juice, tossing to coat well. Place over medium-low heat and cook, stirring occasionally, for 6-8 minutes until apples soften. Remove from the heat. Strain any excess liquid and discard. Stir the stem ginger with syrup, marmalade, sultanas and half the biscuits into the apples. Cool.
 Lay 2 filo sheets on a bench, slightly overlapping to form a 30cm x 45cm rectangle. Brush with butter and sprinkle with 1 tbs biscuits. Repeat until you have 5 layers (10 sheets total). Spread apple mixture lengthways down one long side of the pastry, about 4cm in and leaving 4cm at each end. Fold in the ends, then carefully roll up into a sausage shape. Place strudel, seam-side down, on a lined baking sheet. Brush top with butter. Bake for 30 minutes or until golden.
 Remove strudel from oven and transfer to a platter. Dust with icing sugar, then serve hot with ginger custard.
* Stem ginger and ginger marmalade are from delis and selected supermarkets. We used mild-flavoured Duchy Original Ginger Biscuits, from gourmet shops. If using regular gingernut biscuits, halve the quantity as the flavour is stronger. **d.**

Apple & ginger strudel

Lemon delicious

puddings

129 date & chestnut pudding
129 lemon delicious
129 almond croissant pudding
130 sussex pond pudding
130 apple & berry sponge pudding
133 steamed marmalade pudding
133 chocolate bread & butter pudding

Almond croissant pudding

Date & chestnut pudding

puddings.

date & chestnut pudding
Serves 6-8

1 cup (150g) plain flour
1 tsp baking powder
³/₄ tsp ground allspice
1 cup (160g) chopped pitted dates
100g almond meal
1 tbs golden syrup, plus extra to drizzle
1 cup (230g) unsweetened chestnut puree*
¼ cup (60ml) milk
225g unsalted butter
1 firmly packed cup (220g) brown sugar
3 eggs, plus 2 extra yolks
Thick cream or vanilla ice cream, to serve

Grease a 1.5L pudding basin. Line base with a circle of baking paper cut to fit.
 Sift flour, baking powder and allspice into a large bowl. Add dates, toss to coat well, then transfer to a plate, shaking excess flour back into bowl. Stir almond meal through flour mixture and set aside.
 Whisk together syrup, chestnut puree and milk until smooth. Set aside.
 Beat butter and sugar in an electric mixer on medium speed for 5 minutes until thick and pale. Add eggs and extra yolks one at a time, beating well after each addition, until combined. Pour in chestnut mixture, beating, then gradually incorporate flour mixture until a smooth batter. Fold in dates, then pour into basin.
 Cut a 30cm-square piece of baking paper and a 30cm-square piece of foil. Place paper on foil and fold to make a pleat in centre. Place over basin, foil-side up, then tie securely around rim with kitchen string. Place basin in a large pan and fill with enough boiling water to come two-thirds of the way up sides of the basin. Simmer, covered and topping up with water if needed, on medium heat for 3 hours or until a skewer inserted in the centre comes out clean but is still slightly sticky.
 Remove basin from pan and cool for 10 minutes. Carefully turn out onto a serving plate, drizzle with extra syrup, then slice and serve warm with cream or ice cream.
* From delis and gourmet food shops.

lemon delicious
Serves 4-6

70g unsalted butter, softened
Finely grated zest and juice of 2 lemons
1½ cups (330g) caster sugar
3 eggs, separated
¼ cup (35g) self-raising flour, sifted
1½ cups (375ml) milk
Thick cream, to serve

Preheat the oven to 180°C. Grease a 1.5L baking dish.
 Place the butter, zest and sugar in the bowl of an electric mixer and beat until thick and pale. Add the egg yolks, one at a time, beating well after each addition. Transfer to a large bowl. Fold in the flour and beat in the milk and lemon juice until a smooth batter forms.
 Clean the electric mixer and dry well. Beat the eggwhites with a pinch of salt until stiff peaks form. Fold the eggwhite into the batter with a metal spoon, then pour into the prepared dish.
 Place the dish in a roasting pan and pour in enough water to come halfway up the sides of the dish. Bake for 45-50 minutes until the top is golden and just starting to crack, but the bottom remains runny. Remove from the roasting pan and stand for 5 minutes. Serve with thick cream.

almond croissant pudding
Serves 6-8

4 almond croissants (preferably day-old), torn into large chunks
4 eggs
½ cup (110g) caster sugar
300ml milk
300ml pure (thin) cream
1 vanilla bean, split, seeds scraped
Finely grated zest of ½ orange
2 tbs brandy
Creme anglaise and chocolate sauce (see Basics, p 136), to serve
Toasted flaked almonds and seasonal fruit, to decorate
Icing sugar, to dust

Grease the base and sides of a 1L terrine or loaf pan and line with baking paper. Pack the croissants into the terrine or pan, then set aside.
 Whisk the eggs and sugar together in a large bowl until just combined. Place the milk, cream and vanilla pod and seeds in a saucepan over low heat and bring to just below boiling point, then gradually pour the warm milk mixture into the egg mixture, whisking constantly. Add the orange zest and brandy and whisk well to combine, then pour the mixture over the croissants in the pan and stand at room temperature for 1 hour to allow the custard to soak in – this will make for a lighter pudding.
 Preheat the oven to 180°C.
 Bake the pudding for 45 minutes until just set and golden on top (cover with foil if it's browning too quickly). Remove the pudding from the oven, allow to cool slightly, then turn out and slice. Place on a serving platter and drizzle with creme anglaise and chocolate sauce, then scatter with almonds and fruit and serve dusted with icing sugar.

puddings.

Sussex pond pudding

sussex pond pudding
Serves 6

2 lemons (preferably unwaxed, or scrubbed well)
1 2/3 cups (250g) self-raising flour, plus extra to dust
100g vegetable or regular suet*
150ml milk
100g chilled unsalted butter, chopped
1/2 cup (110g) caster sugar
Pure (thin) cream, to serve

Grease a 1.5L pudding basin with butter. Prick the lemons all over with a skewer.

Combine flour and suet in a bowl. Stir in the milk, then knead to form a dough. Shape dough into a rough ball. Cut off one-third and set aside. Roll out the remaining dough on a lightly floured surface to 5mm thick and use it to line the base and side of the pudding basin.

Fill the pudding with half the butter and half the sugar. Place whole lemons on top, then cover with remaining sugar and butter. Roll out remaining dough on a lightly floured surface to 5mm thick. Brush the edges of the pastry case with water. Place pastry over pudding and press edges to seal.

Cut a 30cm square of baking paper and a 30cm square of foil. Place the paper on the foil and fold to make a pleat in the centre (this gives the pudding room to expand). Grease the baking paper side, then place over the basin, foil-side up, and tie with kitchen string to secure.

Place in a large pan. Pour in enough boiling water to come two-thirds up side of basin. Bring to the boil, then reduce heat to medium-low, cover and steam for 3½ hours, topping up with more boiling water if necessary. Remove and set aside for 10 minutes. Turn out onto a plate, then slice and serve warm with cream.
* Vegetable suet is available from health food shops. Regular suet is from the baking aisle at supermarkets.

apple & berry sponge pudding
Serves 6

3 Granny Smith apples, peeled, chopped
2 tsp grated lemon zest plus 2 tbs juice
1 1/2 cups (330g) caster sugar
500g frozen mixed berries
2 eggs
2 tbs milk
1 tsp vanilla extract
1 cup (150g) plain flour, sifted with 1 tsp baking powder
Icing sugar, to dust
Thick cream mixed with 1 tsp ground cinnamon, to serve

Preheat the oven to 180°C. Place the apple, lemon juice and 1 cup (220g) sugar in a small saucepan and cook over low heat, stirring, for 3 minutes or until the sugar dissolves. Cook for a further 3-4 minutes, stirring occasionally, until apple softens slightly. Stir through berries. Transfer to a 1.25L baking dish and set aside.

Beat eggs, milk and remaining 1/2 cup (110g) sugar with an electric beater until pale. Add vanilla, then fold in the flour and baking powder to combine. Spread the mixture over the fruit, then bake in the oven for 20-25 minutes or until risen and golden. Dust with icing sugar and serve with cinnamon cream.

Apple & berry sponge pudding

Steamed marmalade pudding

puddings.

steamed marmalade pudding
Serves 6

150g suet* (or chilled unsalted butter, grated)
2 cups (140g) fine, fresh white breadcrumbs
½ cup (110g) caster sugar
2 tsp orange blossom water*
Grated zest of 1 orange
2 eggs, lightly beaten
⅓ cup (80ml) milk
200g Seville orange marmalade or other orange marmalade
60g self-raising flour
Custard or cream, to serve

Grease a 1.5L pudding basin with butter.

Place the suet, breadcrumbs and sugar in a bowl and combine well. Stir in orange blossom water, zest and eggs. Stir in milk and half the marmalade. Sift in the flour and stir well until a stiff mixture forms.

Spoon the remaining marmalade into the bottom of the pudding basin, then add the pudding mixture.

Cut a 30cm square of baking paper and a 30cm square of foil. Place paper on the foil and fold to make a pleat in the centre (this gives the pudding room to expand). Grease the baking paper side, then place over the basin, foil-side up, and tie the rim with kitchen string to secure.

Place an inverted saucer in the base of a large pan and sit the pudding basin on top. Pour in enough boiling water to come halfway up the side of the basin. Bring to the boil over high heat, then cover with a tight-fitting lid. Reduce the heat to low and allow to simmer for 2½ hours – check the pan occasionally as you may need to top up with more boiling water if necessary. Remove and set aside for 10 minutes. Turn out, cut into slices and serve with custard.

* Suet is from supermarkets. Orange blossom water is from gourmet food shops and selected supermarkets.

Chocolate bread & butter pudding

chocolate bread & butter pudding
Serves 6

16 slices spicy fruit bread
30g unsalted butter, softened
⅓ cup (80ml) Pedro Ximénez sherry* or rum
120g good-quality dark chocolate, broken into pieces
1 cup (250ml) milk
1 cup (250ml) pure (thin) cream, plus extra to serve
2 eggs
½ cup (110g) caster sugar
1 tsp vanilla extract
Icing sugar, to dust

Preheat the oven to 170°C. Grease a square 1.2L baking dish.

Toast the bread, then spread one side with the butter and cut the slices in half. Overlap the bread in the prepared baking dish to make 2 layers. Drizzle with the sherry.

Place the chocolate in a saucepan with the milk and cream and gently cook over medium heat, stirring, until the chocolate melts.

In a bowl, whisk the eggs, caster sugar and vanilla extract together until combined. Stir in the chocolate mixture, then pour over the bread and leave for 10 minutes to soak.

Bake for 35 minutes (the filling will still be slightly runny), then stand for 5 minutes. Dust the pudding with icing sugar and serve with extra cream.

* Pedro Ximénez is a sweet Spanish sherry, available from bottle shops. **d.**

SUBSCRIBE OR EXTEND NOW:

- Receive 11 issues for only $65 – save 22% off the regular cover price
- Enjoy convenient, free delivery to your home or office each month
- Never miss an issue
- Protect yourself from future cover price rises
- It's the perfect gift that lasts all year

To subscribe, go to **magsonline.com.au/del/X540**

Subscribe & save
Pay only $65 for one year

Each month, the award-winning *delicious.* magazine brings you fresh, simple recipes from all your favourite chefs, so you don't want to miss an issue. Subscribe now or extend your current subscription and you'll receive 11 issues for just $65 – that's a saving of 22 per cent!

Yes, I would like to subscribe to *delicious*:

SUBSCRIPTION OPTIONS:

Me	Gift				
☐	☐	1 year (11 issues)	Australia	$65	**(SAVE 22%)**
☐	☐	2 years (22 issues)	Australia	$121	**(SAVE 27%)**
☐	☐	1 year (11 issues)	New Zealand	A$72	
☐	☐	1 year (11 issues)	Overseas	A$155	

☐ I already subscribe. Please extend my subscription with the term selected above.

MY DETAILS:

Mrs/Ms/Miss/Mr _____
Address _____
Postcode _____ Daytime telephone _____
Email _____ DOB _____

GIFT RECIPIENT DETAILS:

Mrs/Ms/Miss/Mr _____
Address _____
Postcode _____ Daytime telephone _____
Email _____

Please send a card to announce my gift to: ○ Me ○ Gift recipient

PAYMENT DETAILS:

Cheque/money order for $ _____ is enclosed payable to News Magazines
or charge $ _____ to: ○ Visa ○ Mastercard ○ Amex ○ Diners Club

Card number

☐☐☐☐ ☐☐☐☐ ☐☐☐☐ ☐☐☐☐

Cardholder's signature _____ Expiry date __/__
Cardholder's name (please print) _____

SUBSCRIBING IS EASY

🖱 **magsonline.com.au/del/X540**

☎ **1300 656 933 and quote X540**
Overseas and mobiles, tel: +61 (0)2 8296 5424
Fax: +61 (0)2 9279 3161

✉ Send original or copy of this coupon (no stamp required) to:
News Magazines, Reply Paid 1224, Queen Victoria Building NSW 1229

magsonline

OFFER ENDS SEPTEMBER 30, 2011

Offer is open to Australian residents only and ends September 30. By including your email address, *delicious*. will keep you informed of offers and updates from News Magazines, and specially selected partners.

Please tick if you'd prefer to miss out on offers and updates from:
☐ News Magazines ☐ Our specially selected partners

or call 1300 656 933 and quote X540

basics.

beef stock
1kg beef or veal bones
2 tbs olive oil
2 onions, quartered
2 garlic cloves, unpeeled
2 celery stalks & 2 leeks (white part only), chopped
1 carrot, chopped
2 tbs tomato paste
Bouquet garni, made from 2 bay leaves and 2 sprigs each parsley and thyme, tied together with kitchen string

Preheat oven to 200°C. Place the bones, in a single layer, on a baking tray. Drizzle with the oil and roast for 30 minutes. Add the vegetables and return to the oven for a further 1 hour, turning once or twice.

Transfer to a large stockpot. Add the tomato paste and bouquet garni and cover with 4L water. Bring to the boil over high heat, then reduce the heat to low and simmer, uncovered, for 4 hours. Strain stock into a bowl. Cool. Chill overnight.

Use a metal spoon to skim any fat from surface. Place stock in a saucepan and return to the boil. Reduce heat to low and simmer for a further 20 minutes to concentrate the flavour before using. (Alternatively, cool, then keep in the fridge for up to 5 days, or frozen for 3 months.) Makes 2L.

chicken stock
1.6kg whole chicken or 1kg chicken wings, rinsed
1 large onion, quartered
1 leek (white part only), chopped
3 celery stalks, quartered
2 garlic cloves, bruised
2 bay leaves
1 tsp whole black peppercorns

Place all ingredients in a stockpot with 1 tbs sea salt and cover with water. Cover with a lid, then bring to a boil over medium-high heat. Turn chicken and reduce heat to medium-low. Simmer, uncovered, skimming foam from surface, for $1\frac{1}{2}$ hours or until meat falls from the bone. Remove chicken. Strain stock through a muslin-lined sieve, discarding solids. Use immediately. (Alternatively cool, then keep in the fridge for up to 5 days, or frozen for 3 months.) Makes 2L.

cheese pastry
$2\frac{1}{3}$ cups (350g) plain flour, plus extra to dust
$\frac{1}{3}$ cup (55g) coarse polenta
150g chilled unsalted butter, chopped
$\frac{3}{4}$ cup (60g) grated parmesan

Place the flour, polenta, butter and a pinch of salt in a food processor and process until the mixture resembles breadcrumbs. Transfer to a bowl, add 50g of parmesan, then stir with a knife to combine. Gradually stir in $\frac{1}{3}$ cup (80ml) cold water until dough just comes together (you may not need all the water). Turn dough out onto a floured surface and gently knead until dough comes together in a ball. Enclose in plastic wrap and chill for 20 minutes. Makes a deep 23cm pie.

roasted tomato sugo
2kg vine-ripened tomatoes, halved
1 garlic bulb, cloves separated (skin on)
1 rosemary sprig
2 sprigs each basil, oregano and thyme
$\frac{1}{4}$ cup (60ml) olive oil
2 tbs balsamic vinegar
2 tsp caster sugar

Preheat oven to 180°C. Place tomatoes on a baking tray with garlic, herbs, oil and balsamic. Sprinkle with sugar. Season and toss to coat. Turn tomatoes cut-side up. Roast for 1 hour or until tomatoes and garlic are softened. Cool. Peel tomatoes and garlic (the skin will slip off easily). Discard herb stalks. Whiz in a processor to a coarse puree. Season. Store in an airtight container in the fridge for 1 week or frozen for 3 months. Makes 1.5L.

chocolate sauce
300g good-quality dark chocolate, chopped
300ml pure (thin) cream

Place the chocolate in a heatproof bowl. Place the cream in a saucepan over medium heat and bring to just below boiling point. Pour over the chocolate, then stir until smooth. Serve warm, or cool before storing in the fridge for up to 1 week. Makes 600ml.

creme anglaise
4 egg yolks
1 cup (250ml) milk
300ml pure (thin) cream
$\frac{1}{4}$ cup (55g) caster sugar
1 tsp vanilla extract

Lightly beat yolks in a bowl. Place milk, cream, sugar and vanilla in a pan over medium heat and bring to just below boiling point. Pour hot milk mixture over yolks, whisking constantly, then return to pan over very low heat. Stir constantly with a wooden spoon for 5-6 minutes until thick enough to coat back of spoon. Pour into a jug, cover surface closely with plastic wrap to prevent a skin forming, then chill. Makes $2\frac{1}{2}$ cups.

starters & light meals

Blue cheese, onion &
  pine nut focaccia (v) 23
Cauliflower cheese soup (v) 16
Chicken, barley & vegetable soup 12
Duck rillettes 24
Fennel soup with winter greens
  and bacon 15
Homestyle minestrone 11
Hot and sour prawn soup 19
Mexican chilli con carne soup 15
Mini tapas (v) 27
Moroccan spiced soup with
  jewelled couscous 19
Mulled pear salad with
  roquefort dressing (v) 23
Pea, ham & sausage soup 16
Ploughman's soup 12
Roast capsicum & tomato soup (v) 11
Thai-style butternut pumpkin soup
  with prawns 11
Vodka-cured salmon with
  watercress pancakes 27
Warm pumpkin
  & goat's cheese salad (v) 23
Winter ceviche of kingfish and salmon ...24

mains

Aromatic duck curry 93
Baked lamb & apricot couscous 59
Beef Wellington pie 36
Braised veal shanks with
  Sicilian olives and gremolata 44
Beef, stout & potato pies 39
Butternut, spinach &
  goat's cheese pie (v) 36
Cauliflower pasta 82
Chargrilled vegetable, mozzarella
  & prosciutto pasta bake 85
Cheesy pumpkin & pasta bake 85
Chicken & asparagus green curry 97
Chicken biryani 89
Chicken korma pies 31
Chicken laksa 94
Chicken, mushroom & Taleggio torta 39
Chicken tagine with preserved lemon 47
Chickpea & chorizo stew 60
Chickpeas with winter vegetables
  and saffron (v) 43
Chilli for a crowd 90
Coconut lamb curry 89
Creamy bacon, leek & pea farfalle 82
Creamy chicken, leek & bacon pie 35
Creamy pot-roast chicken 70
Duck breast ragu with soft polenta 48
Easy fish tagine 93
Fillet steak with quick red wine sauce 64
Fondue-style macaroni cheese 60
Greek lamb with crispy potatoes 70
Greek pasta bake (pasticcio) 101
Lamb & rosemary hotpots 32
Lamb biryani 102
Lamb paprikash 43
Lemon & bacon spatchcocks
  with bread sauce 69
Mexican polenta cobbler 105
Mushroom & bacon risotto 64
Oven-baked risotto with prosciutto
  and fontina 101
Oven-baked sausages and
  balsamic tomatoes 102
Pasta with garlic prawns 78
Perfect potato gnocchi (v) 78
Pork goulash with paprika yoghurt 44
Prawn, watercress & salmon pie 31
Prosciutto-wrapped ocean trout
  with roast kumara 63
Pumpkin & ricotta ravioli with
  chestnut butter sauce (v) 81
Pumpkin, sage & ricotta lasagne (v) 77
Rack of pork with cider apples 69
Red-cooked beef with gai lan 94
Rigatoni with sausage & fennel ragu 77
Roast chicken with peas and bacon 59
Roast duck with star anise
  & orange sauce 73
Rogan josh-braised chicken 90
Rosemary salt-roast lamb with
  boulangère potatoes 73
Satay pork pies 31
Sausage & lentil braise 47
Sausage & porcini mushroom
  cannelloni 105
Sausage pasty 32
Sausages and champ mash with
  eschalot gravy 59
Slow-cooked lamb with
  parsley dumplings 48
Spaghetti puttanesca 81
Spaghetti with spicy bolognese 77
Spiced kumara pies with
  yoghurt pastry (v) 35
Spiced meatball curry 63
Spicy baked eggs (v) 101
Thai pork larb 97
Thyme-roasted rib of beef with
  red wine gravy 69
Traditional beef daube 43

side dishes & basics

Baby vegetables (v) 109
Baked creamy celeriac and
  potato gratin (v) 114
Beef stock 136
Caponata (v) 114
Cheese & potato bake (tartiflette) 113
Cheese pastry (v) 136
Chicken stock 136
Chocolate sauce (v) 136
Creme anglaise (v) 136
Field mushrooms stuffed with
  Taleggio and prosciutto 110
Indian spiced eggplant (v) 89
Pan-fried brussels sprouts with
  bacon and almonds 109
Roasted tomato sugo (v) 136
Twice-roasted potatoes with onion,
  herbs and chilli (v) 109
'Wild weed' salad with
  parmesan crisps (v) 113
Whole baked pumpkin 110

(v) denotes vegetarian dishes

desserts

Almond croissant pudding 129
Apple & berry sponge pudding 130
Apple & ginger strudel 124
Cardamom custard tarts 124
Chocolate banoffee pies 119
Chocolate bread & butter
  pudding 133
Date & chestnut pudding 129
Deep-dish apple, sour cream
  & nutmeg pie 123
Lemon delicious 129
Limoncello meringue pies 123
Old-fashioned cherry pie 119
Red & white pear tart 119
Steamed marmalade pudding 133
Sussex pond pudding 130
Treacle pecan tarts 120
Walnut tart with prunes
  in Armagnac 120

index.

delicious.

Editor-in-chief Trudi Jenkins
Food Director Valli Little
Creative Director Scott Cassidy
Managing Editor Danielle Oppermann
Project Editor Molly Furzer
Designers Jacqui Porter, Shannon Keogh, Stephanie Westcott
Subeditors Shannon Harley, Alison Pickel
Food Assistants Jessica Brook Phoebe Wood

Sales Director, Food Amy Copley
Group National Advertising Manager David Rogers
Production Director Mark Moes
Production Manager Neridah Burke
Group Marketing Director, Food Scott Williams
Marketing Manager Kate Grant
Brand Manager Tobi Cornwell
Rights & Syndication Manager Elizabeth Hachem

Chief Executive Officer Sandra Hook
Chief Operating Officer Tim Sligo
Commercial Director Zara Curtis
Finance Director Nicole Tannock
Group Publisher, Food Fiona Nilsson
Group Editorial Director Karen McCartney
Publisher, ABC Magazines Lesley O'Brien
Publishing Editor, ABC Magazines Skye Healey
Publishing Manager, ABC Commercial Liz White

Editorial Enquiries (02) 8062 2791, delicious@newsmagazines.com.au
Subscription Enquiries 1300 656 933

Recipes: All recipes by Valli Little, except: Olivia Andrews (p 44, 48, 129), Kate Belcher (p 44, 69, 101, 102), Angela Boggiano (p 63, 77, 102), Jessica Brook (p 15), Anna Burges-Lumsden (p 31, 32, 35, 36, 81, 82), Phillippa Cheifitz © Woolworths Taste Magazine, South Africa, lifestylefeatures.com (p 12, 35), Matthew Drennan (p 16, 19, 73), Nancy Duran (p 101), Maranda Engelbrecht © Woolworths Taste Magazine, South Africa, lifestylefeatures.com (p 124), Silvana Franco (p 82), Alice Hart (p 19), Sal Henley (p 93), Ching-He Huang (p 94), Lucy Jessop (p 64, 85), Lizzie Kamenetzky (p 90, 133), Debbie Major (70, 93, 105, 123), Tom Norrington-Davies (p 43, 114, 119, 130), Louise Pickford (p 63), Annie Rigg (p 24), Simon Rimmer (p 81), Lizzie Webb-Wilson (p 94, 114), Lucy Williams (p 47, 70, 89, 101, 120), Phoebe Wood (p 11)

Photography: Steve Baxter (p 15, 16, 19, 44, 114), Steve Brown (p 31, 44, 48, 59, 70, 129), Peter Cassidy (p 73), Stephen Conroy (p 69, 129), Neil Corder © Woolworths Taste Magazine, South Africa, lifestylefeatures.com (p 124), Ben Dearnley (p 11, 23, 27, 32, 59, 60, 64, 90, 97, 119, 133), Laura Edwards (p 35), Jonathan Gregson (p 43, 114, 130), Dan Jones (p 70, 47), Richard Jung (p 24, 82), Amanda McLauchlan (p 16, 39, 60, 110, 124), Lis Parsons (p 47, 73, 93, 101, 105, 119), Dirk Pieters © Woolworths Taste Magazine, South Africa, lifestylefeatures.com (p9, 15) Shane Powell © Woolworths Taste Magazine, South Africa, lifestylefeatures.com (p 12, 35), Emma Reilly (p 69, 110), Craig Robertson (p 31, 32, 36, 77, 94, 101, 102), Mark Roper (p 12, 23, 24, 27, 89, 109, 113, 119), Simon Scarboro © Woolworths Taste Magazine, South Africa, lifestylefeatures.com (p 69), Maja Smend (p 90, 120, 133), Brett Stevens (p 23, 31, 39, 43, 48, 77, 85, 97, 109, 113, 120, 129, 130), Petrina Tinslay (p 123), Ian Wallace (p 11, 63, 78, 101), Phillip Webb (p 93), Stuart West (p 64, 81, 82, 85, 89, 94), Kate Whitaker (p 63, 81), Jenny White (p 19), Rob White (p 101)

Styling: Julz Beresford (p 16, 39, 59, 60, 101, 110, 124), Jo Carmichael (p 31, 133), Morag Farquhar (p 19, 31, 32, 36, 44, 47, 81, 82, 93, 105, 119), Yael Grinham (p 31), Lisa Harrison (p 35, 47, 70, 77), Lucy Jessop (p 82), Rachel Jukes (p 64, 73, 81, 85, 94), Lucy McKelvie (p 77, 114), David Morgan (p 12, 23, 24, 27, 31, 39, 43, 59, 69, 70, 77, 85, 89, 90, 97, 109, 113, 119, 129, 130), Kim Morphew (p 16), Michelle Noerianto (p 78), Louise Pickford (p 11, 63, 78), Sue Rowlands (p 73), Polly Webb-Wilson (p 89, 90, 120, 133), Kristen Wilson (p 11, 32, 44, 48, 64, 123, 129)

Editorial enquiries: Locked Bag 5030, Alexandria, NSW 2015, tel: (02) 8062 2791, email: delicious@newsmagazines.com.au. Melbourne Office, HWT Tower, Level 5, 40 City Rd, Southbank, Vic 3006, tel: (03) 9292 2000, fax: (03) 9292 1695. delicious. is published by News Magazines Pty Ltd (ACN 088 923 906), 170-180 Bourke St, Alexandria, NSW 2015, tel: (02) 8062 2666, fax: (02) 8062 2611. News Magazines Pty Ltd is a wholly owned subsidiary of News Limited (ACN 007 871 178). Copyright 2010 by News Magazines Pty Ltd. All rights reserved. "ABC" and the "Wave" device trademark are used under licence from the Australian Broadcasting Corporation. Printed by Toppan Printing Co, China. Colour separations Sinnott Bros. Distributed by Newsagents Direct Distribution (NDD), tel: (02) 9353 9711. No material may be reproduced without prior written permission of the publisher.

ISBN 978-0-9806846-5-0